The HAPPY BABY Cookbook

The HAPPY BABY Cookbook

THE AUSTRALIAN Women's Weekly

contents

Of all the delights and challenges

you face in your life, nothing is as extraordinary as having a child. You will experience many changes, physically and emotionally, some exciting, some unnerving, and all of them unfamiliar. It is easy to feel overwhelmed by these emotions – the unconditional love, overpowering sense of protectiveness, sheer exhaustion and confusion over what is the 'right' way of bringing up your baby.

You want to ensure your child gets a nutritionally balanced diet but you can find yourself overwhelmed by an avalanche of information about feeding. How long you should sustain breastfeeding, whether you should be bottle-feeding, when and what solids to introduce are all questions that can expose new parents to a merry-go-round of advice from well meaning friends and family.

The important thing to remember in the midst of all the conflicting advice is to relax and stay calm. Different methods work for different children, so try to resist the urge to compare your child's eating habits to another child. Trust your instincts.

The brand new world of feeding a baby can be a confusing and lonesome place. If your child isn't feeding well it's all too easy to lose confidence. It's completely natural that the issues around feeding your baby will become a serious preoccupation and can create major anxiety for parents. Whether you are offering the breast or the bottle, it's common to find yourself totally focussed on the feeding habits of your baby.

It's important to remember that there really are no strict patterns, and whatever routine you may develop can easily and suddenly vanish before your eyes. Your child's needs are constantly evolving and keeping up with the fast pace of change is just one of the many lingering challenges of parenthood. Babies who fed voraciously for the first six months might become picky eaters once they start on solids. Babies who began life as delicate little eaters can develop big appetites. Making sure that your child gets all the nourishment he needs can be a source of anxiety and frustration. It's natural to feel like throwing your lovingly created meal against the wall when your little angel rejects it. We've all been there. The key is to try to relax and trust that it could all be a different story next week.

The advice about how, what and when to feed your child has changed drastically over the years. Not long ago mothers were encouraged to start their babies on solid foods at an alarmingly young age, in some cases when they were as young as six weeks, when their little digestive systems were not ready to cope. These days, doctors and health professionals agree that it is best for you to wait until your baby is at least four to six months old before introducing solids. For most babies, breastmilk or formula is all they need until that age, however, for some babies with tremendous appetites and astonishing growth, you may need to start them on solids slightly earlier. If you are in any doubt, always check with your doctor or early childhood centre.

It is especially recommended to hold off introducing solids until six months if there is any family history of allergies, asthma or food intolerances. Australia has one of the highest rates of allergies in the developed world and over the past few decades, there has been an increase in the incidence of food allergies, asthma and eczema in children younger than 5 years old. The foods that are most commonly attributed to causing allergic reactions are milk, egg, peanuts, tree nuts, gluten and shellfish. It is important to be aware of all of these food allergens and to introduce them slowly. Peanut and other nut products shouldn't be introduced before 12 months, or for children with a strong family history of a food allergy, all nut products should be avoided until after 3 years of age. Honey has also been known to contain bacteria that may be harmful to young digestive systems and is not recommended for children under one year old.

When you do start introducing solids, keep it simple and begin with very small quantities. You should begin with rice cereal mixed with breastmilk or formula for the first few weeks, gradually increasing the amount. Remember that your baby is only accustomed to liquids, so make sure the blend is quite runny. When these feeds are going smoothly you can progress to mashed or puréed vegetables and fruits in much the same way. Start out with tiny amounts and work up to larger quantities. When introducing your baby to new foods watch carefully for any signs of a reaction or allergy. And don't get disheartened by an initial adverse reaction to a certain food. Babies opt for familiar foods, so an initial refusal to eat a certain food is not a sure sign that he doesn't like it. Persevere. It can be frustrating, and messy, but you may need to try that food ten times before your baby decides he likes it. And when he does, it's thrilling to see the delight on his face.

It's essential to try the full range of puréed vegetables and fruits to see which ones your baby really likes, as well as to ensure that he is getting the right balance of nutrients that he needs to grow up to be strong and healthy. Children begin developing their eating habits from day one, and that's why it's so important that you start them on the right foot. By making family meals healthy and nutritious right from the beginning, you are setting them up for a lifetime of healthy food choices. This book is designed to ease the stress and help you to make those healthy food choices for your family.

food for pregnant women

Pregnancy often brings with it

a good excuse to overindulge. In fact, many mothers feel they'd be neglecting their baby's nutritional needs if they didn't. But the eating for two idea is simply a myth. In reality, you only need 300 extra calories a day when you're pregnant, and fewer in your first trimester.

Make sure you don't drink alcohol or smoke and that you eat plenty of whole grains, vegetables and fruits. You also need a folate-rich diet, especially in the very early stages of pregnancy so it's a good idea to increase your folate intake while trying to conceive. Folate is crucial to the healthy development of babies and is found in leafy green vegetables, wholegrain breads, cereals and legumes such as peas, dried beans and lentils.

Certain foods are considered to be harmful during pregnancy. These include soft and semi-soft cheeses, raw seafood and meats, smoked fish and various types of bean sprouts. Check with your health professional about the foods to avoid when you are pregnant.

corn fritters

1 cup (150g) self-raising flour
½ teaspoon bicarbonate of soda
1 teaspoon ground cumin
¾ cup (180ml) milk
2 eggs, separated
2 cups (330g) fresh corn kernels
2 green onions, sliced finely
2 tablespoons finely chopped fresh coriander

You can substitute 425g can corn kernels, rinsed and drained, for the fresh corn kernels, if you like.

1 Sift flour, soda and cumin into medium bowl. Gradually whisk in milk and egg yolks until batter is smooth.
2 Beat egg whites in small bowl with electric mixer until soft peaks form.
3 Stir corn, onion and coriander into batter; fold in egg whites.
4 Pour 2 tablespoons of the batter for each fritter into heated oiled large frying pan; spread batter into round shape. Cook fritters about 2 minutes each side. Remove from pan; cover to keep warm.
5 Repeat step 4 to make a total of 18 fritters. Fritters can be served with tomato chutney and fresh coriander leaves, if you like.

prep + cook time 40 minutes **makes** 18

Little Miss Muffet

Little Miss Muffet, sat on a tuffet,
Eating her curds and whey.
Along came a spider,
Who sat down beside her
And frightened Miss Muffet away.

bircher muesli with figs and pistachios

1½ cups (135g) rolled oats
¼ cup (30g) oat bran
¼ cup (15g) natural bran flakes
¾ cup (180ml) milk
¾ cup (180ml) orange juice
¾ cup (200g) low-fat greek-style yogurt
½ cup (100g) finely chopped dried figs
½ teaspoon ground cinnamon
½ cup (70g) roasted pistachios, chopped coarsely
1 large orange (300g), segmented

1 Combine cereals, milk, juice, yogurt, figs and cinnamon in large bowl. Cover; refrigerate overnight. Stir in half the nuts.

2 Divide muesli among serving bowls; top with orange segments and remaining nuts.

prep + cook time 15 minutes (+ refrigeration) **serves** 4

creamy scrambled eggs

8 eggs
½ cup (125ml) cream
2 tablespoons finely chopped fresh chives
30g butter

1 Place eggs, cream and chives in medium bowl; beat lightly with fork.

2 Heat butter in large frying pan over medium heat. Add egg mixture, wait a few seconds, then use a wide spatula to gently scrape the set egg mixture along the base of the pan; cook until creamy and set. Serve immediately, with toast, if you like.

prep + cook time 25 minutes **serves** 4

chicken, pea and asparagus soup with pistou

3 cups (750ml) chicken stock
3 cups (750ml) water
1 clove garlic, crushed
¼ teaspoon coarsely ground black pepper
400g chicken breast fillets
170g asparagus, trimmed, chopped coarsely
1½ cups (240g) shelled fresh peas
1 tablespoon lemon juice

pistou
½ cup coarsely chopped fresh flat-leaf parsley
½ cup coarsely chopped fresh mint
¼ cup coarsely chopped fresh garlic chives
2 teaspoons finely grated lemon rind
1 clove garlic, crushed
2 teaspoons olive oil

1 Bring stock, the water, garlic and pepper to the boil in large saucepan. Add chicken; return to the boil. Reduce heat; simmer, covered, about 10 minutes or until chicken is cooked through. Cool in poaching liquid 10 minutes. Remove chicken from pan; slice thinly.
2 Meanwhile, make pistou.
3 Add remaining ingredients to soup; bring to the boil. Return chicken to pan; simmer, uncovered, about 3 minutes or until vegetables are just tender.
4 Divide soup among serving bowls; top with pistou.
pistou Using mortar and pestle, pound ingredients until smooth.

prep + cook time 30 minutes serves 4

chickpea ratatouille

2 tablespoons olive oil
1 medium red onion (170g), cut into thin wedges
2 cloves garlic, crushed
1 medium eggplant (300g), chopped coarsely
1 medium red capsicum (200g), chopped coarsely
2 medium zucchini (240g), sliced thickly
400g can chickpeas, rinsed, drained
4 small egg tomatoes (240g), chopped coarsely
2 tablespoons tomato paste
½ cup (125ml) water
⅔ cup loosely packed fresh basil leaves

1 Heat half the oil in large frying pan; cook onion and garlic, stirring, about 5 minutes or until onion softens. Remove from pan.
2 Heat remaining oil in same pan; cook eggplant, capsicum and zucchini, stirring, about 5 minutes or until eggplant is browned lightly.
3 Return onion mixture to pan with chickpeas, tomato, paste and the water; simmer, covered, about 10 minutes or until vegetables soften. Remove from heat; stir in basil.

prep + cook time 35 minutes serves 4

Pistou is a Provençal term, derived from a French word that means to pound. Similar in appearance to the Italian pesto, pistou is traditionally made with fresh herbs, olive oil and garlic. You need 450g of fresh peas in the pod or 2 cups (240g) frozen peas for this recipe.

Humpty Dumpty

Humpty Dumpty
sat on a wall.
Humpty Dumpty
had a great fall.
All the king's horses
and all the king's men
Couldn't put Humpty
together again.

tomato-stuffed avocado halves

2 large avocados (640g)
2 large tomatoes (440g), seeded, chopped finely
1 small red onion (100g), chopped finely
2 tablespoons olive oil
2 tablespoons lime juice
2 tablespoons finely chopped fresh coriander
¼ teaspoon Tabasco sauce

1 Halve avocados; remove and discard seeds. Using a large spoon, carefully remove avocado flesh from skin in one piece; discard skin.
2 Combine remaining ingredients in small bowl.
3 Serve avocado halves topped with tomato mixture.

prep time 20 minutes **serves** 4

broccoli and garlic breadcrumb spaghetti

12 slices stale white bread
500g spaghetti
300g broccoli, cut into florets
⅓ cup (80ml) olive oil
50g butter
2 cloves garlic, crushed
¼ cup (20g) shaved parmesan cheese

1 Remove and discard crusts from bread; process bread until fine.
2 Cook pasta in large saucepan of boiling water until tender; drain.
3 Meanwhile, boil, steam or microwave broccoli until tender; drain.
4 Heat oil and butter in large frying pan; cook breadcrumbs and garlic until browned lightly and crisp.
5 Combine pasta, broccoli and breadcrumbs in a large bowl. Serve sprinkled with shaved parmesan.

prep + cook time 25 minutes **serves** 4

red lentil patty salad

1 cup (200g) red lentils
¼ cup (40g) burghul
½ cup (125ml) boiling water
1 small brown onion (80g), chopped coarsely
2 cloves garlic, quartered
⅔ cup (100g) plain flour
1 egg
1 cup (100g) packaged breadcrumbs
2 tablespoons olive oil
1 cup loosely packed fresh flat-leaf parsley leaves
3 medium tomatoes (450g), cut into wedges
1 lebanese cucumber (130g), chopped coarsely
1 medium avocado (250g), chopped coarsely
1 small green capsicum (150g), sliced thinly

lemon yogurt dressing

1 cup (280g) yogurt
2 teaspoons finely grated lemon rind
2 tablespoons lemon juice

1 Cook lentils in medium saucepan of boiling water until tender; drain, cool.
2 Meanwhile, place burghul in small heatproof bowl; cover with the water. Stand 10 minutes.
3 Blend or process lentils, onion and garlic until smooth; transfer to medium bowl. Stir in burghul, flour, egg and breadcrumbs. Refrigerate 1 hour or until firm.
4 Meanwhile, make lemon yogurt dressing.
5 Shape lentil mixture into 20 patties. Heat oil in large frying pan; cook patties until browned. Drain on absorbent paper.
6 Combine patties with remaining ingredients in large bowl; drizzle with dressing.

lemon yogurt dressing Combine ingredients in small bowl.

prep + cook time 20 minutes (+ cooling & refrigeration) **serves** 4

Broccolini is a cross between broccoli and chinese kale. It has long, asparagus-like stems and long loose florets, both of which are edible. It resembles broccoli in look, but is milder and sweeter.

chicken, mixed vegies and almond stir-fry

2½ cups (500g) jasmine rice
2 tablespoons vegetable oil
600g chicken breast fillets, sliced thinly
1 medium brown onion (150g), sliced thinly
2 cloves garlic, crushed
350g broccolini, trimmed, chopped coarsely
115g fresh baby corn, halved lengthways
150g sugar snap peas, trimmed
⅓ cup (45g) roasted slivered almonds
1 tablespoon fish sauce
1 tablespoon sweet chilli sauce

1 Cook rice in large saucepan of boiling water, uncovered, until just tender; drain. Cover to keep warm.
2 Meanwhile, heat half the oil in wok; stir-fry chicken, in batches, until browned lightly and cooked through.
3 Heat remaining oil in wok; stir-fry onion and garlic until onion softens. Add broccolini, corn and peas; stir-fry until vegetables are tender.
4 Return chicken to wok with nuts and sauces; stir-fry until heated through. Serve with rice.

prep + cook time 30 minutes **serves** 4

beef and bean casserole

2 tablespoons olive oil
1kg beef chuck steak, cut into 2cm pieces
2 medium brown onions (300g), chopped finely
2 cloves garlic, crushed
1 teaspoon ground turmeric
2 teaspoons ground cumin
½ teaspoon dried chilli flakes
¼ cup (70g) tomato paste
410g can crushed tomatoes
2 cups (500ml) beef stock
2 bay leaves
2 medium potatoes (400g), chopped coarsely
400g can kidney beans, rinsed, drained
¼ cup coarsely chopped fresh coriander
¼ cup coarsely chopped fresh flat-leaf parsley

Recipe is suitable to freeze at the end of step 3.

1 Heat oil in large saucepan; cook beef, in batches, until browned.
2 Add onion and garlic to pan; cook, stirring, until onion softens. Add spices; cook, stirring, until fragrant. Add paste; cook, stirring, 1 minute.
3 Return beef to pan with undrained tomatoes, stock and bay leaves; bring to the boil. Reduce heat; simmer, covered, 1 hour.
4 Add potato to pan; simmer, uncovered, about 30 minutes or until potato is tender.
5 Discard bay leaves. Add beans to pan; stir until heated through. Remove from heat, stir through herbs.

prep + cook time 2 hours 20 minutes **serves** 4

grilled moroccan lamb with burghul salad

¾ cup (120g) burghul
1 tablespoon olive oil
1 tablespoon ras el hanout
800g lamb backstraps
½ cup (70g) roasted unsalted pistachios, chopped coarsely
1 small red onion (100g), chopped finely
¾ cup loosely packed fresh parsley leaves
¾ cup loosely packed fresh mint leaves
⅓ cup (55g) dried currants
1 tablespoons finely grated lemon rind
1 clove garlic, crushed
¼ cup (60ml) lemon juice
2 tablespoons olive oil, extra

1 Place burghul in medium bowl, cover with water. Stand 10 minutes; drain. Squeeze out as much excess water as possible.
2 Combine oil, spice and lamb in medium bowl, turn to coat lamb in mixture. Cook lamb, in batches, on heated oiled grill plate (or grill or barbecue) until browned both sides and cooked as desired. Cover lamb; stand 10 minutes then slice thickly.
3 Combine burghul in medium bowl with remaining ingredients; toss gently.
4 Serve salad topped with sliced lamb and, if you like, yogurt.

prep + cook time 40 minutes **serves** 4

shepherd's pie

30g butter
1 medium brown onion (150g), chopped finely
1 medium carrot (120g), chopped finely
½ teaspoon dried mixed herbs
4 cups (750g) finely chopped cooked lamb
¼ cup (70g) tomato paste
¼ cup (60ml) tomato sauce
2 tablespoons worcestershire sauce
2 cups (500ml) beef stock
2 tablespoons plain flour
⅓ cup (80ml) water

potato topping
5 medium potatoes (1kg), chopped coarsely
60g butter
¼ cup (60ml) milk

1 Preheat oven to 200°C/180°C fan-forced. Oil shallow 2.5-litre (10-cup) ovenproof dish.
2 Make potato topping.
3 Meanwhile, heat butter in large saucepan; cook onion and carrot, stirring, until tender. Add mixed herbs and lamb; cook, stirring, 2 minutes. Stir in paste, sauces and stock, then blended flour and water; stir over heat until mixture boils and thickens. Pour mixture into dish.
4 Drop heaped tablespoons of potato topping onto lamb mixture. Bake in oven about 20 minutes or until browned and heated through.

potato topping Boil, steam or microwave potato until tender; drain. Mash with butter and milk until smooth.

prep + cook time 1 hour **serves** 4

With a name that loosely translates as "top of the shop", ras el hanout is an aromatic Moroccan blend of the best a spice merchant has to offer: allspice, cumin, paprika, fennel, caraway and saffron are all generally part of the mix. It is available from Middle Eastern and specialty spice stores.

breast or bottle?

Choosing whether to breastfeed

or formula-feed your baby is one of the first decisions you'll make as a new parent. Your decision may be influenced by your personal beliefs, your birthing experience or the medical advice you receive.

In an ideal world all mothers would breastfeed, as there are many compelling advantages for both the mother and baby. It is what nature intended for babies, the perfect first food that contains all your baby's nutritional needs with a delicate balance of the proteins, fats and carbohydrates necessary for your baby's development. It helps defend against infections and diseases, helps prevent allergies, optimises brain development and protects against a number of chronic conditions. And not only that, but it is also easily served, whenever needed, and requires no fussy sterilisation techniques or heating beforehand. Many mothers find that breastfeeding their baby is one of life's most rewarding experiences and are happy that they are able to lovingly provide their baby with such a wonderful start in life.

Can't breastfeed? Relax

For many legitimate reasons, sometimes a mother is simply unable to breastfeed her baby. Many women in this situation will experience feelings of shame, guilt and inadequacy, not to mention frustration. It is important to remember that at the end of the day, being relaxed and happy is the most important thing you can do for your baby, doing so will have a positive effect on both of you.

Fabulous formula

You can also take comfort in the fact that infant formulas are the closest thing to mother's milk available, and are scientifically formulated to meet all your baby's nutritional needs. There can also be many advantages to bottle-feeding. Bottle-feeding brings with it the flexibility for your partner, family and friends to share the pleasure of feeding your baby. Many fathers love and look forward to the opportunity to feed their baby, and it means that they can experience the bonding that feeding brings. Bottle-feeding also means that you know exactly how much your baby is eating. It is essential that all bottle-feeding equipment is thoroughly sterilised after feeds. You also need to ensure that the formula you are using is appropriate for your baby's needs and that the size of the teat is correct for your baby, otherwise you may have trouble getting him to feed.

Get some sleep while you can

This is an incredibly exhausting and demanding time for parents. The first few months can be particularly energy depleting. Your baby will not distinguish between night and day; it's all just one big 24-hour cycle of feeding and sleeping. It's so important that mothers try to sleep when their babies do, otherwise functioning as a normal human being becomes a sleep-deprived dream of the past. Feeding around the clock is exhausting, but should begin to ease a little between six and eight weeks. If after eight weeks you are still feeding around the clock then consult your early childhood centre. They will be able to offer advice and encouragement, and the support that you need.

Breastfeeding

Breastfeeding is a skill that both mothers and babies have to learn. This news often comes as shock to those who presume it will be easy and natural. It requires patience and practice. But once you've both got the hang of it, your baby should suck well and the milk should flow smoothly. There is no right or wrong routine here, whatever works for you and your baby is the right way. Just like adults, some babies are slower eaters and others slurp it up in record time. Either way they are getting the goodness of your breast milk, which changes to meet their changing nutritional needs. And the action of sucking and swallowing from the nipple is important for the development of your baby's jaw. You should breastfeed for at least the first 4-6 months. Some particularly hungry babies will need to start being introduced to solids from four months, but most babies will start after six months.

Bottle-feeding

Bottle-feeding your baby is a reliable alternative to breastfeeding that will not hinder your child's health or development. To optimise the bonding process when you bottle-feed, hold your baby close to your chest, as if you are breastfeeding. Most babies like the formula warmed to room temperature, which can be most easily done by placing the bottle in a jug of boiled water. Microwaving is another way but is more risky because it can easily overheat the milk.

Bottle-feeding requires six bottles and matching teats, as well as sterilising equipment. You'll need to disinfect your baby's bottles for the first 12 months of their life while their immune system is still developing. Wash the bottles out first using hot soapy water, then rinse in hot water and then sterilise.

Preparing infant formula involves placing scoops of the formula powder into cooled, boiled water in the bottle. Make sure you always use the correct proportion of scoops for amount of water, as per the instructions. It's worthwhile having a supply of pre-boiled water (in sealed, sterile bottles) on hand at all times. When you go out, the best way to transport formula is to take a supply of pre-boiled water and powdered formula in separate containers and mix them when required.

first foods

Introducing your baby to solids

is an exciting experience, but it can also be harrowing at times. The trick is to keep it simple and begin with tiny quantities. Babies should start out with very small amounts of rice cereal mixed with breastmilk or formula, and then when these feeds are running smoothly move onto vegetable and fruit purées. Start on these much the same way, with very small quantities and work up to larger amounts.

A hand held blender is the best investment you could make while puréeing foods for your baby. It purées small quantities and is quick and easy to clean up. If you want to blend larger quantities at a time, a good way to store it is in ice cube trays in the freezer. You can then pop out a couple of cubes at a time for your baby's meal.

purées made easy

The tables on the next few pages have been created so you can quickly and easily make your purée of choice, according to the groupings of fruit or vegetable. Read down the first column on the left of each table to find your ingredient of choice, then read across to discover the quantity you'll need, the preparation technique and the time it will take to cook. For a purée that could be slightly gluggy, we've also suggested what quantity of liquid you'll need to add to make it easier for your baby to manage.

fruit purées

Fruit and vegetable purées can be frozen in 1-tablespoon batches in ice-cube trays, covered, for up to 1 month.

for apple and pear:

1 Combine fruit and the water in medium saucepan; bring to the boil. Reduce heat; simmer, uncovered, until tender.

2 Blend or process fruit mixture until smooth. Give your child as much fruit purée as desired.

for remaining fruit:

Blend or process fruit until smooth. Give your child as much fruit purée as desired.

all purées make 1 cup (12 tablespoons)

fruit	quantity	preparation	cooking time	water
apple	2 large (400g)	peel, core, chop coarsely	10 minutes	2 tablespoons
avocado	2 small (400g)	peel, seed, chop coarsely	-	-
banana	2 medium (400g)	peel, chop coarsely	-	-
custard apple	400g	peel, seed, chop coarsely	-	-
pear	1 large (330g)	peel, core, chop coarsely	20 minutes	2 tablespoons
rockmelon	500g	peel (remove all green sections), seed, chop coarsely	-	-

apple
pear
avocado
banana
custard apple
rockmelon

carrot
cauliflower
spinach
patty-pan squash
kumara
pumpkin
potato
broccoli
zucchini

vegetable purées

When puréeing vegetables, you can add breastmilk, formula or water to achieve desired consistency.

for potato and pumpkin:

1 Steam vegetable until tender; drain.
2 Push vegetable through sieve.

for remaining vegetables:

Steam vegetable until tender; drain. Blend or process vegetable (and liquid) of choice until smooth. Give your child as much vegetable purée as desired.

all purées make 1 cup (12 tablespoons)

vegetable	quantity	preparation	cooking time	liquid
broccoli	250g	cut into florets, chop stem coarsely	8 minutes	2 tablespoons
carrot	2 large (360g)	trim ends, peel, chop coarsely	15 minutes	2 tablespoons
cauliflower	250g	trim stem, cut into florets	8 minutes	-
kumara	1 medium (400g)	peel, chop coarsely	20 minutes	1 tablespoon
potato	2 medium (400g)	peel, chop coarsely	20 minutes	2 tablespoons
pumpkin	400g	peel, remove seeds, chop coarsely	12 minutes	-
spinach	250g	trim stems, chop coarsely	8 minutes	1 tablespoon
squash, patty-pan	300g	trim ends, chop coarsely	12 minutes	-
zucchini	2 large (300g)	trim ends, peel, chop coarsely	7 minutes	-

purée combinations

All of the purée combinations on these pages are made using the completed fruit and vegetable purées that feature on the previous pages (38-41).

all combinations make ¼ cup (3 tablespoons)

potato and pumpkin

Combine 2 tablespoons puréed potato with 1 tablespoon puréed pumpkin.

potato and spinach

Combine 2 tablespoons puréed potato with 1 tablespoon puréed spinach.

kumara and squash

Combine 2 tablespoons puréed kumara with 1 tablespoon puréed squash.

carrot and broccoli

Combine 2 tablespoons puréed carrot with 1 tablespoon puréed broccoli.

carrot and spinach

Combine 2 tablespoons puréed carrot with 1 tablespoon puréed spinach.

apple and avocado

Combine 2 tablespoons puréed apple with 1 tablespoon puréed avocado.

Use ripe peaches for the peach and raspberry purée as under-ripe fruit will give a sour-tasting purée.

You will need 2 passionfruit for the banana and rockmelon purée. This recipe is not suitable to freeze.

peach and raspberry purée

2 medium ripe peaches (300g), halved
¼ cup (60ml) water
125g fresh or frozen raspberries

1 Preheat oven to 180°C/160°C fan-forced.
2 Place peaches, cut-side down, in ovenproof dish; add the water. Roast about 15 minutes or until peaches are tender; cool. Discard skin.
3 Blend or process peaches and raspberries until smooth. Push mixture through sieve into small bowl.

prep + cook time 25 minutes (+ cooling) **makes** 1 cup (12 tablespoons)

banana and rockmelon purée

1 tablespoon passionfruit pulp
100g piece ripe rockmelon, chopped coarsely
½ medium ripe banana (100g), chopped coarsely

1 Push passionfruit through sieve over small bowl; discard seeds.
2 Blend or process remaining ingredients with passionfruit juice until smooth.

prep time 10 minutes **makes** ⅔ cup

apple and blueberry purée

2 large red apples (400g), peeled, cored, chopped coarsely
½ cup (75g) frozen blueberries
1 tablespoon water

1 Combine ingredients in small saucepan; bring to the boil. Reduce heat; simmer, covered, about 10 minutes or until fruit is tender.
2 Blend or process mixture until smooth. Push through sieve.

prep + cook time 20 minutes **makes** 1 cup

apple with rice cereal

1 tablespoon brown rice flour
1 cup (250ml) water
2 large apples (400g), chopped coarsely

1 Blend brown rice flour with the water in small saucepan; stir over heat until mixture boils and thickens. Cool to room temperature.
2 Meanwhile, boil, steam or microwave apple until tender; drain, push through sieve into small bowl.
3 Combine 1 tablespoon rice cereal with 1 tablespoon apple purée to serve.

prep + cook time 15 minutes (+ standing) **makes** 1 cup rice cereal; 1 cup apple purée

apricot purée with rice cereal

⅔ cup (100g) dried apricots
1½ cups (375ml) water
2 tablespoons rice cereal
⅓ cup (80ml) formula or breast milk, warmed

1 Combine apricots and water in small pan; simmer, covered, about 20 minutes or until apricots are tender. Blend apricots and cooking liquid until smooth.
2 Mix cereal in small bowl with breast milk or formula; serve topped with 1 tablespoon apricot purée.

prep + cook time 25 minutes **makes** ⅓ cup rice cereal; 1¼ cups apricot purée

apple and blueberry purée

We used red apples in the apple and blueberry purée as green apples are often too tart for infants. Golden delicious apples can also be used (for both apple recipes). They are very sweet.

apple with rice cereal

apricot purée with rice cereal

banana with semolina

You need to give babies and young children very ripe bananas. Those that are even slightly green can give a child a severe tummy ache.

pear and date purée

chicken, zucchini and parsnip purée

banana with semolina

2 teaspoons ground semolina
⅓ cup (80ml) water
1 small overripe banana (130g)

1 Blend semolina and the water in small saucepan; stir over heat until mixture boils and thickens. Cool to room temperature.
2 Push banana through sieve into small bowl.
3 Combine 1 tablespoon semolina with 1 tablespoon banana purée to serve.

prep + cook time 15 minutes (+ standing)
makes ⅓ cup semolina; 2½ tablespoons banana purée

pear and date purée

2 medium pears (460g), peeled, chopped coarsely
3 fresh dates (60g), seeded, chopped coarsely
¼ cup (60ml) water

1 Combine ingredients in small saucepan; bring to the boil. Reduce heat; simmer, covered, about 10 minutes or until fruit is tender.
2 Blend or process mixture until smooth. Push mixture through sieve into small bowl.

prep + cook time 20 minutes **makes** 1 cup

chicken, zucchini and parsnip purée

1 single chicken breast fillet (170g), chopped coarsely
2 small zucchini (180g), chopped coarsely
1 small parsnip (120g), chopped coarsely
1¼ cups (310ml) water

1 Place ingredients in small saucepan; bring to the boil. Boil, uncovered, until vegetables soften and chicken is cooked through.
2 Blend or process mixture until smooth.

prep + cook time 30 minutes **makes** 2 cups

yogurt snacks

mango and passionfruit yogurt

Blend or process ½ cup yogurt and ¼ small coarsely chopped ripe mango until smooth. Serve yogurt drizzled with 2 teaspoons passionfruit pulp.

prep time 5 minutes **serves** 1

banana and maple yogurt

Combine ½ cup yogurt and ½ teaspoon maple syrup in small bowl. Serve yogurt topped with ½ small thinly sliced ripe banana and another ½ teaspoon maple syrup.

prep time 5 minutes **serves** 1

apple yogurt with cinnamon

Peel and coarsely grate ½ small fresh apple, then chop coarsely. Combine apple with ⅓ cup yogurt, 1 tablespoon sultanas and tiny pinch ground cinnamon in small bowl. Sprinkle with a little ground cinnamon, if you like.

prep time 5 minutes **serves** 1

yogurt with dried fruit and coconut

Combine 1 tablespoon finely chopped dried apricots, 1 tablespoon finely chopped raisins and 1 teaspoon desiccated coconut in small bowl. Place ⅓ cup yogurt in serving bowl; sprinkle with apricot mixture.

prep time 5 minutes **serves** 1

honey yogurt

Combine 1 teaspoon honey and 1 cup natural or vanilla yogurt in small bowl.

prep time 5 minutes
makes about 1 cup

Honey may contain harmful bacteria and is not recommended for children under one year old.

beef, carrot and kumara purée

150g beef rump steak, diced into 3cm pieces
½ small kumara (125g), chopped coarsely
1 large carrot (180g), chopped coarsely
1½ cups (375ml) water

1 Place ingredients in small saucepan; bring to the boil. Boil, uncovered, until vegetables soften and beef is cooked through.
2 Blend or process mixture until smooth.

prep + cook time 30 minutes **makes** 2 cups

avocado and cucumber purée

1 large ripe avocado (320g), chopped coarsely
1 lebanese cucumber (130g), peeled, seeded, chopped coarsely

1 Blend or process ingredients until smooth.

prep time 5 minutes **makes** 1 cup

fish, potato and spinach purée

1 large potato (300g), chopped coarsely
1½ cups (375ml) water
100g firm white fish fillet, chopped coarsely
30g baby spinach leaves
¼ cup (60ml) water, extra

1 Place potato and the water in small saucepan; bring to the boil. Boil, uncovered, until potato is tender; strain potato over small bowl.
2 Return liquid to same pan with fish and spinach; boil, uncovered, until fish is cooked through. Drain.
3 Push potato through sieve into small bowl. Blend or process fish and spinach until smooth; stir fish mixture and the extra water into potato.

prep + cook time 30 minutes **makes** 2 cups

beef, carrot and kumara purée

Freeze any unused fish purée in 1-tablespoon batches in ice-cube trays, covered, for up to 1 month. Make sure any skin and bones have been removed from the fish before cooking.

The avocado purée is not suitable to freeze, as it will discolour when thawed.

avocado and cucumber purée

fish, potato and spinach purée

potato, kumara and parsnip purée

Little Boy Blue

Little Boy Blue,
come blow your horn,
The cow's in the meadow,
the sheep's in the corn.
Where is the boy
who looks after the sheep?
He's under a haystack,
fast asleep.
Will you wake him? No, not I,
For if I do, he's sure to cry.

cauliflower, broccoli and cheese purée

dhal purée

potato, kumara and parsnip purée

1 small kumara (250g), chopped coarsely
1 small potato (120g), chopped coarsely
1 small parsnip (120g), chopped coarsely
1 tablespoon water

1 Steam vegetables until tender; drain.
2 Push vegetables through sieve into small bowl; stir in the water.

prep + cook time 30 minutes **makes** 1 cup

cauliflower, broccoli and cheese purée

100g cauliflower, chopped coarsely
150g broccoli, chopped coarsely
¼ cup (30g) coarsely grated cheddar cheese
2 tablespoons water

1 Steam vegetables until tender; drain.
2 Blend or process vegetables, cheese and the water until smooth. Push through sieve.

prep + cook time 20 minutes **makes** ¾ cup

dhal purée

¾ cup (180ml) water
200g pumpkin, chopped coarsely
1 small carrot (70g), chopped coarsely
1 small zucchini (90g), chopped coarsely
2 tablespoons red lentils

1 Combine ingredients in small saucepan; bring to the boil. Reduce heat; simmer, uncovered, about 15 minutes or until vegetables and lentils are tender.
2 Blend or process mixture until smooth. Push through sieve.

prep + cook time 25 minutes **makes** 1 cup

chicken, corn and risoni purée

100g chicken breast fillet, chopped coarsely
1¼ cups (310ml) water
1 cup (160g) fresh or frozen corn kernels
1 tablespoon risoni pasta

1 Combine ingredients in small saucepan; bring to the boil. Reduce heat; simmer, uncovered, about 10 minutes or until pasta is tender and chicken is cooked through.
2 Blend or process mixture until smooth. Push through sieve.

prep + cook time 25 minutes **makes** 1 cup

fish chowder purée

1 teaspoon olive oil
1 tablespoon finely chopped rindless bacon
¼ stalk celery (35g), trimmed, chopped coarsely
½ cup (125ml) hot milk
1 baby new potato (40g), chopped finely
50g firm white fish fillet, chopped coarsely
3 coarsely chopped fresh chives

This recipe is not suitable to freeze.

1 Heat oil in small saucepan; cook bacon and celery, stirring, until celery softens. Add milk and potato; bring to the boil. Simmer, uncovered, stirring occasionally, about 8 minutes or until potato is tender. Add fish; simmer, uncovered, about 2 minutes or until cooked through.
2 Blend or process fish mixture and chives until smooth.

prep + cook time 25 minutes **makes** ½ cup

If using fresh kernels in the chicken, corn and risoni purée, you will need about 1 trimmed corn cob (250g) for this recipe.

Jack Sprat

Jack Sprat could eat no fat,
His wife could eat no lean,
And so, between them both you see,
They licked the platter clean.

veal mince and bean purée

1 teaspoon olive oil
120g veal mince
½ cup (130g) bottled tomato pasta sauce
¼ cup (50g) rinsed, drained, canned butter beans
3 fresh flat-leaf parsley sprigs
1 tablespoon water

1 Heat oil in small frying pan; cook mince, stirring, about 5 minutes or until cooked through. Add sauce; bring to the boil. Reduce heat; simmer, uncovered, about 3 minutes or until thickened.
2 Blend or process veal mixture with remaining ingredients until smooth. Push through sieve.

prep + cook time 15 minutes **makes** 1 cup

ratatouille purée

2 teaspoons olive oil
1 large zucchini (150g), chopped coarsely
1 baby eggplant (60g), chopped coarsely
½ cup (130g) bottled tomato pasta sauce
2 tablespoons water
2 fresh basil leaves

1 Heat oil in medium saucepan; cook zucchini and eggplant, stirring, 5 minutes. Add sauce and the water; bring to the boil. Reduce heat; simmer, covered, about 15 minutes or until vegetables soften.
2 Blend or process tomato mixture with basil until smooth. Push through sieve.

prep + cook time 25 minutes **makes** 1 cup

vegetable mash made easy

The tables on the next few pages have been created so you can quickly and easily make your mash of choice, according to the groupings of fruit or vegetable. Read down the first column on the left of each table to find your ingredient of choice, then read across to discover the quantity you'll need, the preparation technique and the time it will take to cook. For a mash that could be slightly gluggy, we've also suggested a quantity of liquid to add to make it easier for your baby to manage.

You can boil or microwave the asparagus, beans, parsnip and peas, if you prefer. Freeze any unused mash in 1-tablespoon batches in ice-cube trays, covered, for up to 1 month.

for asparagus, beans, parsnip and peas:

1 Steam vegetable until tender; drain.

2 Blend, process or mash vegetable (and liquid) until desired consistency.

Give your child as much vegetable mash as desired.

for button mushrooms:

1 Melt 20g butter in medium frying pan; cook mushrooms, stirring, until tender.

2 Blend, process or mash mushrooms until desired consistency. Give your child as much vegetable mash as desired.

for cabbage:

1 Place cabbage, stock and the water in medium saucepan; cook, stirring, until tender.

2 Blend, process or mash cabbage until desired consistency. Give your child as much vegetable mash as desired.

for leek:

1 Melt 20g butter in large frying pan; cook leek, stirring, 5 minutes. Add stock; cook, stirring, about 5 minutes or until leek is tender.

2 Blend, process or mash leek until desired consistency. Give your child as much vegetable mash as desired.

all mash recipes make 1 cup (12 tablespoons)

vegetable	quantity	preparation	cooking time	liquid
asparagus	300g	trim, chop coarsely	5 minutes	-
beans	300g	trim, chop coarsely	10 minutes	-
button mushroom	300g	chop finely	5 minutes	-
cabbage	¼ small (300g)	chop finely	5 minutes	⅓ cup salt-reduced vegetable stock and ⅓ cup water
leek	1 medium (350g)	chop coarsely	10 minutes	½ cup salt-reduced vegetable stock
parsnip	1 large (350g)	peel, chop coarsely	15 minutes	2 tablespoons milk
peas (frozen)	250g	-	5 minutes	1 tablespoon water

fruit mash

Freeze any unused mash in 1-tablespoon batches in ice-cube trays, covered, for up to 1 month.

for apple and prune:

1 Combine apple, prune and the water in medium saucepan; bring to the boil. Reduce heat; simmer, covered, until apple and prune are tender.

2 Blend, process or mash apple mixture until desired consistency. Give your child as much fruit mash as desired.

for blueberry:

1 Combine blueberries and the water in medium saucepan; bring to the boil. Reduce heat; simmer, uncovered, until softened.

2 Push blueberries through sieve in small bowl. Give your child as much fruit mash as desired.

for strawberry:

1 Combine strawberries and juice in medium saucepan; bring to the boil. Reduce heat; simmer, uncovered, until softened.

2 Push strawberries through sieve in small bowl. Give your child as much fruit mash as desired.

for remaining fruits:

1 Blend, process or mash fruit (and liquid) until desired consistency. Give your child as much fruit mash as desired.

all mash recipes make 1 cup (12 tablespoons)

fruit	quantity	preparation	cooking time	liquid
apple and prune	2 large apples (400g) ⅓ cup (55g) seeded prunes	apple: peel, core, slice thinly prunes: chop coarsely	15 minutes	¼ cup water
apricot	425g can, drained	-	-	-
blueberry	300g	chop coarsely	5 minutes	2 tablespoons water
grape (seedless)	250g	chop coarsely	-	-
mandarin	2 medium (400g)	peel, discard pith, seed	-	1 tablespoon apple juice
mango	2 small (600g)	peel, seed, chop coarsely	-	-
papaya	1 small (650g)	peel, seed, chop coarsely	-	-
peach	425g can, drained	-	-	-
strawberry	375g	chop coarsely	5 minutes	¼ cup apple juice

mash combinations

All of the mash combinations on these pages are made using the completed fruit and vegetable mashes that feature on the previous pages (60-63).

all combinations make ⅓ cup (4 tablespoons)

vegetable and cheese

Combine 1 tablespoon mashed asparagus, 1 tablespoon mashed parsnip and 1 tablespoon mashed pea; top with 1 tablespoon finely grated tasty cheese.

leek and mushroom

Combine 3 tablespoons mashed leek with 1 tablespoon mashed mushroom.

fruit yogurt

Combine 1 tablespoon mashed strawberry, 1 tablespoon mashed blueberry and 2 tablespoons natural or vanilla yogurt.

pumpkin and sweet corn

Combine 2 tablespoons mashed canned creamed corn with 2 tablespoons puréed pumpkin (see page 41).

peach and apricot

Combine 2 tablespoons mashed apricot with 2 tablespoons mashed peach.

Add a little cold milk to the porridge just before serving if it is too thick.

For the risoni, freeze the vegetable mixture in ¼-cup batches, covered, for up to 1 month.

oat porridge

⅓ cup (80g) rolled oats
¾ cup (180ml) milk

1 Combine ingredients in small saucepan; bring to the boil.
2 Reduce heat; simmer, uncovered, about 8 minutes or until all liquid is almost absorbed. Cool.

prep + cook time 15 minutes **makes** ½ cup

risoni with mixed vegetables

1 small red capsicum (150g), chopped finely
1 large zucchini (150g), chopped finely
310g can corn kernels, drained
400g can crushed tomatoes
2 tablespoons risoni pasta

1 Cook capsicum in medium heated lightly oiled non-stick frying pan, stirring, 3 minutes. Add zucchini and corn; cook, stirring, 2 minutes. Add undrained tomatoes; cook, stirring occasionally, about 15 minutes or until vegetables soften. Blend or process until smooth.
2 Meanwhile, cook risoni in small saucepan of boiling water, uncovered, until tender; drain.
3 Toss risoni with ¼ cup of the vegetable mixture.

prep + cook time 20 minutes **makes** ⅓ cup risoni; 1½ cups vegetable mixture

creamy cheese polenta

1 cup (250ml) water
1½ cups (375ml) milk
⅓ cup (55g) polenta
¼ cup (30g) coarsely grated cheddar cheese

1 Combine the water and milk in small saucepan; bring to the boil. Gradually add polenta to liquid, stirring constantly.
2 Reduce heat; simmer, stirring, about 10 minutes or until polenta thickens. Stir in cheese, cover; cool 10 minutes, stirring occasionally.

prep + cook time 20 minutes (+ standing) **makes** 1 cup

scrambled egg

1 egg
2 tablespoons milk
5g butter

1 Combine egg and milk in small bowl.
2 Heat butter in small frying pan; cook egg mixture, stirring, over low heat, until egg sets.

prep + cook time 5 minutes **makes** ⅓ cup

tofu and vegetable patties

1 tablespoon mashed silken tofu
1 tablespoon mashed kumara
1 tablespoon mashed carrot
1 tablespoon puréed zucchini
2 teaspoons rice flour

1 Combine ingredients in small bowl; shape into two patties.
2 Heat small lightly oiled non-stick frying pan; cook patties, uncovered, about 3 minutes each side or until heated through and browned lightly.

prep + cook time 20 minutes **makes** 2

creamy cheese polenta

scrambled egg

Any leftover mashed vegetables can be used to make the tofu and vegetable patties, just be sure to use a total of ¼ cup (3 tablespoons) of mash along with the 2 teaspoons of rice flour.

tofu and vegetable patties

Cheese sauce can also be used on mashed vegetables, puréed chicken or pasta. Freeze remaining cheese sauce in 1-tablespoon batches in ice-cube trays, covered, for up to 1 month.

You can freeze the remaining soup in 1-tablespoon batches in ice-cube trays, covered, for up to 2 months.

fish in cheese sauce

10g butter
2 teaspoons plain flour
½ cup (125ml) milk
2 tablespoons finely grated cheddar cheese
30g flathead fillet
1 tablespoon small broccoli florets

1 Melt butter in small saucepan, add flour; cook, stirring, until mixture bubbles and thickens. Gradually add milk; cook, stirring, until sauce boils and thickens slightly. Remove from heat; stir in cheese.
2 Meanwhile, boil, steam or microwave fish and broccoli, separately, until broccoli is tender and fish is cooked through; drain.
3 Flake fish into small chunks, carefully removing any bones; combine fish, broccoli and 1 tablespoon of the cheese sauce in small bowl.

prep + cook time 20 minutes **makes** 1 cup cheese sauce

pumpkin and kumara soup

1 tablespoon olive oil
1 small brown onion (80g), chopped coarsely
1 clove garlic, chopped coarsely
200g pumpkin, chopped coarsely
1 small kumara (250g), chopped coarsely
½ cup (125ml) salt-reduced chicken stock
½ cup (125ml) milk
½ cup (125ml) water

1 Heat oil in small saucepan; cook onion and garlic, stirring, until onion softens. Add pumpkin, kumara and stock; cook, covered, over medium heat, about 15 minutes or until pumpkin and kumara are tender.
2 Blend or process pumpkin mixture until smooth. Return to pan with milk and the water; bring to the boil. Reduce heat; simmer, uncovered, 5 minutes or until soup is heated through.

prep + cook time 45 minutes **makes** 2 cups

baked ricotta with tomato sauce

400g ricotta cheese
1 tablespoon finely chopped fresh oregano
1 tablespoon olive oil
1 clove garlic, crushed
425g can diced tomatoes
½ cup (130g) bottled tomato pasta sauce
1 teaspoon white sugar

1 Preheat oven to 160°C/140°C fan-forced. Line oven tray with baking paper.
2 Using hand, combine cheese and oregano in small bowl; shape mixture into four patties. Place on tray; drizzle with half of the oil. Bake, uncovered, about 20 minutes or until heated through.
3 Meanwhile, heat remaining oil in small saucepan; cook garlic, stirring, 1 minute. Add undrained tomatoes, pasta sauce and sugar; bring to the boil. Reduce heat; simmer, uncovered, stirring occasionally, about 15 minutes or until sauce thickens. Serve sauce with baked ricotta.

prep + cook time 30 minutes **makes** 4

chicken livers with pumpkin

200g chicken livers
½ cup (125ml) milk
500g pumpkin, chopped coarsely
1 tablespoon olive oil

1 Soak livers in milk in small bowl 30 minutes; drain, discard milk. Separate livers into halves by cutting lobes apart.
2 Meanwhile, boil, steam or microwave pumpkin until just tender; drain.
3 Heat oil in medium frying pan; cook livers, over high heat, about 5 minutes or until cooked through. Drain on absorbent paper.
4 Blend or process pumpkin and livers until smooth, or mash with a fork.

prep + cook time 15 minutes (+ standing) **makes** 2 cups

Leftover baked ricotta can be used in pasta, a frittata or on pizza.

For the chicken livers with pumpkin, if the mixture is too thick, add a little water to obtain desired consistency.

eating with the family

Welcoming your bundle of joy

to the family dining table is a delightful and unifying experience for the family. It also means that you don't need to prepare different meals for your family and your baby, essentially halving your time in the kitchen. As soon as babies can eat solid food they can start to eat family food, but you will need to adapt some things to make it suitable for your baby. The food must be chopped very finely and be mildly spiced, but you can always add more fiery ingredients such as chilli or wasabi once you have taken out the amount needed for the baby. Also, you should go easy on the salt, which can easily be added at the table if needed.

The flavours, spice levels and ingredients in these recipes are designed to be suitable for the whole family. As toddlers will often eat earlier than adults, it's a good idea to prepare food that can be easily re-heated for the rest of the family. Casseroles, soups, pastas and risottos are all good choices.

roast butterflied chicken with mash and fresh corn

1.6kg chicken
30g butter, softened
1 teaspoon finely chopped fresh thyme
2 teaspoons finely grated lemon rind
3 trimmed corn cobs (750g), quartered

creamy mash
800g potatoes, chopped coarsely
⅔ cup (160ml) warm milk
20g butter

toddler tip Remove kernels from one corn cob quarter and chop them with a small piece of chicken meat. Serve with a few tablespoons of creamy mash.

1 Preheat oven to 220°C/200°C fan-forced.
2 Using kitchen scissors, cut along both sides of backbone of chicken; discard backbone. Place chicken, skin-side up, on board; using heel of hand, press down on breastbone to flatten chicken.
3 Combine butter, thyme and rind in small bowl. Loosen skin of chicken by sliding fingers between skin and meat at the neck joint. Push butter mixture under skin.
4 Place chicken on lightly oiled wire rack in large shallow baking dish; roast, uncovered, about 45 minutes or until chicken is cooked through.
5 Meanwhile, make creamy mash. Boil, steam, or microwave corn until tender; drain.
6 Serve chicken with corn and creamy mash.

creamy mash Boil, steam or microwave potato until tender; drain. Mash potato in large bowl with milk and butter.

prep + cook time 1 hour **serves** 4

chicken casserole

1 tablespoon olive oil
8 chicken drumsticks (1kg)
1 medium brown onion (150g), chopped coarsely
150g button mushrooms, quartered
2 cloves garlic, crushed
2 tablespoons tomato paste
400g can diced tomatoes
1 cup (250ml) chicken stock
2 sprigs fresh thyme
⅓ cup (70g) bottled char-grilled vegetables, drained, chopped coarsely

cheesy polenta
3 cups (750ml) milk
¾ cup (125g) polenta
¼ cup (20g) finely grated parmesan cheese

You could use mixed char-grilled vegetables from a delicatessen instead of the bottled variety. This recipe is best made just before serving; it's not suitable to freeze as the mushrooms will become tough and rubbery.

1 Preheat oven to 180°C/160°C fan-forced.
2 Heat oil in large flameproof dish; cook chicken, in batches, until browned.
3 Cook onion, mushrooms and garlic in same dish, stirring, until onion softens. Add paste, undrained tomatoes, stock, thyme and chicken; bring to the boil. Cover; transfer to oven, bake 25 minutes. Uncover; bake about 20 minutes or until chicken is cooked through. Remove and discard thyme. Remove some chicken meat from bone for toddler; shred chicken.
4 Meanwhile, make cheesy polenta.
5 Place some of the polenta in small serving bowl; top with toddler's chicken, drizzle with some of the tomato mixture.
6 Add char-grilled vegetables to remaining tomato mixture; season to taste. Divide remaining polenta into serving bowls; top with tomato mixture and remaining chicken.

cheesy polenta Place milk in medium saucepan; bring to the boil. Gradually stir polenta into milk. Reduce heat; simmer, stirring, about 10 minutes or until polenta thickens. Remove from heat, stir in cheese.

prep + cook time 1 hour **serves** 4

lamb cutlets with ratatouille

2 tablespoons olive oil
1 medium red onion (170g), sliced thinly
1 large red capsicum (350g), chopped coarsely
3 large zucchini (450g), sliced thickly
5 baby eggplants (300g), sliced thickly
400g can diced tomatoes
1 tablespoon tomato paste
2 cloves garlic, crushed
12 french-trimmed lamb cutlets (900g)

1 Heat oil in large saucepan; cook onion, capsicum, zucchini and eggplant, stirring, 5 minutes. Add undrained tomatoes and paste; bring to the boil. Reduce heat; simmer, covered, about 20 minutes or until vegetables have softened. Stir in garlic.
2 Meanwhile, cook cutlets on heated oiled grill plate (or grill or barbecue) until cooked as desired. Serve with ratatouille.

prep + cook time 40 minutes **serves** 4

chicken and vegetable soup

2 teaspoons vegetable oil
2 green onions, sliced thinly
1 clove garlic, crushed
2 cups (500ml) chicken stock
2 cups (500ml) water
350g chicken mince
1 tablespoon cornflour
¼ cup (60ml) water, extra
310g can creamed corn
1 cup (160g) fresh corn kernels
100g snow peas, trimmed, sliced thinly
1 egg, beaten lightly

1 Heat oil in large saucepan; cook onion and garlic, stirring, until onion softens. Add stock and the water; bring to the boil. Add chicken, reduce heat; simmer, stirring, about 5 minutes or until chicken is cooked through.
2 Blend cornflour and extra water in small jug; add to pan with creamed corn, corn kernels and snow peas. Cook, stirring, until mixture boils and thickens. Gradually add egg, in thin stream, to soup just before serving.

prep + cook time 30 minutes **serves** 4

For toddlers, cut the meat from one cutlet; trim it of all fat then cut into bite-size pieces and serve with a few tablespoons of mashed ratatouille.

For the soup, purée the toddler portion before adding egg.

lamb stew with buttermilk mash

2 tablespoons olive oil
700g diced lamb
1 medium brown onion (150g), chopped coarsely
1 large carrot (180g), chopped coarsely
2 stalks celery (300g), trimmed, chopped coarsely
2 cups (500ml) beef stock
400g can diced tomatoes
150g button mushrooms, halved
½ cup (60g) frozen peas
½ cup (60g) coarsely grated cheddar cheese

buttermilk mash

4 medium potatoes (800g), chopped coarsely
½ cup (125ml) buttermilk, warmed

The stew is at its best made just before serving, but if you want to freeze the stew, cook it up until the end of step 2. Mushrooms are not freezer friendly. Add the mushrooms after reheating the stew. Thaw the stew in the fridge overnight, or in a microwave oven. The mash will not respond well to freezing either.

1 Heat half the oil in large saucepan; cook lamb, in batches, until browned.

2 Heat remaining oil in same pan; cook onion, stirring, until onion softens. Return lamb to pan with carrot, celery, stock and undrained tomatoes. Bring to the boil. Reduce heat; simmer, covered, 1 hour. Uncover; simmer 30 minutes.

3 Add mushrooms; simmer, uncovered, about 30 minutes or until lamb is tender. Add peas; stir until heated through.

4 Meanwhile, make buttermilk mash.

5 Serve toddler some of the lamb mixture over a little of the buttermilk mash.

6 Preheat grill.

7 Divide remaining lamb mixture into three deep 2-cup ovenproof dishes, season to taste; top with mash, sprinkle with cheese. Grill pies until browned lightly.

buttermilk mash Boil, steam or microwave potato until tender; drain. Mash potato with buttermilk in medium bowl until smooth.

prep + cook time 2 hours 30 minutes **serves** 4

potato and bacon frittata

1 medium potato (200g), chopped coarsely
6 eggs
½ cup (125ml) milk
¼ cup (20g) finely grated parmesan cheese
1 tablespoon finely chopped fresh flat-leaf parsley
2 rindless bacon rashers (130g), chopped coarsely
3 cherry tomatoes, quartered
20g baby rocket leaves

aïoli
⅓ cup (100g) mayonnaise
1 tablespoon buttermilk
1 clove garlic, crushed

You will need a small ovenproof frying pan with an 18cm base for this recipe. If your frying pan does not have a heatproof handle, wrap the entire handle in several thicknesses of aluminium foil before placing it under the grill. Frittata can be eaten warm or cold; it can be made about 12 hours ahead of serving time; keep covered in the fridge. Frittata is not suitable to freeze. The aïoli can be made several days ahead; keep covered in the fridge.

1 Make aïoli.
2 Boil, steam or microwave potato until tender; drain.
3 Combine eggs, milk, cheese and parsley in large jug.
4 Cook bacon in heated oiled medium ovenproof frying pan until browned; drain on absorbent paper. Return bacon to same pan with potato; pour egg mixture into pan. Cook over medium heat about 5 minutes or until frittata is browned underneath and almost set.
5 Meanwhile, preheat grill.
6 Grill frittata about 5 minutes or until browned lightly.
7 Cut a small slice from frittata for toddler; serve with cherry tomatoes.
8 Serve remaining frittata with rocket leaves and aïoli.

aïoli Whisk ingredients in small bowl until smooth.

prep + cook time 35 minutes **serves** 4

Queen of Hearts

The Queen of Hearts,
She made some tarts,
All on a summer's day;
The Knave of Hearts,
He stole those tarts,
And took them clean away.
The King of Hearts
Called for the tarts,
And beat the Knave full sore;
The Knave of Hearts
Brought back the tarts,
And vowed he'd steal no more.

asian grilled chicken with green beans

2 tablespoons hoisin sauce
2 tablespoons lime juice
1 tablespoon soy sauce
2cm piece fresh ginger (10g), grated
1 clove garlic, crushed
6 chicken thigh fillets (660g), halved
400g green beans, trimmed
2 teaspoons peanut oil
2 green onions, sliced thinly
2 tablespoons oyster sauce

1 Combine hoisin, juice, soy, ginger and garlic in medium bowl, add chicken; turn chicken to coat in marinade. Cover; refrigerate 1 hour.
2 Cook drained chicken on heated oiled grill plate (or grill or barbecue) until cooked through.
3 Meanwhile, boil, steam or microwave beans until just tender; drain. Heat oil in medium frying pan; cook beans, onion and oyster sauce, stirring, until heated through.
4 Serve chicken and beans with steamed jasmine rice.

prep + cook time 25 minutes (+ refrigeration) **serves** 4

broccoli and cheese frittata with tomato salad

400g broccoli
1 cup (120g) coarsely grated cheddar cheese
½ cup (40g) coarsely grated parmesan cheese
7 eggs
⅓ cup (80ml) cream

tomato salad
500g cherry tomatoes, halved
200g yellow teardrop tomatoes, halved
½ cup loosely packed baby basil leaves
2 tablespoons balsamic vinegar
1 tablespoon olive oil

toddler tip Don't dress toddler's salad portion.

1 Preheat oven to 180°C/160°C fan-forced. Grease 20cm x 30cm lamington pan. Line base and sides with baking paper.
2 Discard broccoli stalks; thinly slice florets vertically. Place broccoli in large saucepan of boiling water; return to the boil, drain. Rinse under cold water; drain. Pat dry with absorbent paper.
3 Layer broccoli and combined cheeses in prepared pan then pour over combined eggs and cream. Cook, uncovered, in moderate oven about 25 minutes or until frittata sets. Cool 5 minutes.
4 Meanwhile, combine ingredients for tomato salad in medium bowl.
5 Serve frittata with salad.

prep + cook time 40 minutes **serves** 4

oregano chicken kebabs with herb couscous

2 tablespoons finely chopped fresh oregano
2 teaspoons finely grated lemon rind
1 tablespoon lemon juice
2 cloves garlic, crushed
500g chicken tenderloins, chopped coarsely
1 teaspoon ground coriander
½ teaspoon ground cumin
½ teaspoon dried chilli flakes
½ cup (140g) yogurt

herb couscous
⅔ cup (160ml) chicken stock
¾ cup (150g) couscous
2 tablespoons lemon juice
¼ cup finely chopped fresh flat-leaf parsley

Soak the bamboo skewers in water for at least one hour before using to prevent scorching. The chicken can be marinaded overnight, then skewered and cooked close to serving. The marinaded chicken mixture can be frozen for up to 2 months; thaw overnight in the fridge. Couscous is best made just before serving.

1 Combine oregano, rind, juice and garlic in small bowl. Combine a sprinkling of the oregano mixture with a few of pieces of the chicken in a small bowl for the toddler; cover, refrigerate 1 hour.
2 Combine remaining oregano mixture, remaining chicken, spices and chilli in medium bowl; cover, refrigerate 1 hour.
3 Thread chicken for toddler onto one bamboo skewer. Thread remaining chicken onto eight bamboo skewers. Cook skewers on heated oiled grill plate (or grill or barbecue) until cooked.
4 Meanwhile, make herb couscous.
5 Remove chicken for toddler from skewer. Serve chicken with a little of the herb couscous.
6 Season remaining chicken and herb couscous to taste: serve with yogurt.

herb couscous Bring stock to the boil in small saucepan; remove from heat, add couscous and juice. Cover couscous; stand 5 minutes, fluffing with fork occasionally. Stir in parsley.

prep + cook time 40 minutes (+ refrigeration) **serves** 4

chicken, corn and pasta soup

2 teaspoons vegetable oil
2 green onions, sliced thinly
3cm piece fresh ginger (15g), grated
2 cloves garlic, crushed
3 cups (750ml) water
2 cups (500ml) chicken stock
300g chicken breast fillet
420g can creamed corn
½ cup (110g) risoni pasta
1 tablespoon japanese soy sauce
1 baby buk choy (150g), shredded finely

Add some thinly sliced red chilli for a spicy version of this soup, if you like. This is a last minute soup; it doesn't freeze well. The pasta will become soggy as it absorbs more liquid and the buk choy will discolour.

1 Heat oil in large saucepan; cook onion, ginger and garlic, stirring, until onion softens. Add the water and stock; bring to the boil. Add chicken; reduce heat. Simmer, covered, about 10 minutes or until chicken is cooked. Remove from heat; cool chicken in broth 10 minutes. Remove chicken from broth; chop meat finely.
2 Return broth to the boil. Add corn and pasta to pan; simmer, uncovered, about 10 minutes or until pasta is tender. Return chicken to pan; simmer, uncovered, until heated through.
3 Remove some of the soup for toddler to a small bowl.
4 Add sauce and buk choy to remaining soup, season to taste; simmer, uncovered, until buk choy wilts.

prep + cook time 50 minutes **serves** 4

chicken sang choy bow

1 tablespoon peanut oil
700g chicken mince
1 small red capsicum (150g), chopped finely
150g mushrooms, chopped finely
1 clove garlic, crushed
3 green onions, chopped finely
2 tablespoons oyster sauce
2 tablespoons soy sauce
2 tablespoons hoisin sauce
1 teaspoon sesame oil
2 cups (160g) bean sprouts
100g packet fried crunchy noodles
8 large iceberg lettuce leaves
2 green onions, sliced thinly, extra

1 Heat peanut oil in wok; stir-fry chicken until changed in colour.
2 Add capsicum, mushrooms and garlic; stir-fry until vegetables are just tender.
3 Add chopped onion, sauces and sesame oil; stir-fry until chicken is cooked through. Remove from heat; stir in sprouts and noodles.
4 Divide lettuce leaves among serving plates. Spoon chicken mixture into leaves; sprinkle each with sliced onion.

prep + cook time 30 minutes **serves** 4

sausage pasta bake

6 thick beef sausages (480g)
375g penne
1 tablespoon olive oil
1 medium brown onion (150g), chopped coarsely
1 small red capsicum (150g), chopped coarsely
1 small yellow capsicum (150g), chopped coarsely
1 large zucchini (150g), sliced thinly
200g mushrooms, quartered
¼ cup coarsely chopped fresh basil
700g bottled tomato pasta sauce
1 cup (100g) coarsely grated mozzarella cheese
½ cup (40g) coarsely grated parmesan cheese

1 Preheat oven to 200°C/180°C fan-forced.
2 Cook sausages in large heated frying pan until cooked through; cut into 1cm slices.
3 Meanwhile, cook pasta in large saucepan of boiling water, uncovered, until just tender; drain.
4 Heat oil in same cleaned frying pan; cook onion, capsicums and zucchini, stirring, until vegetables are tender. Add mushrooms, basil and pasta sauce; bring to the boil. Reduce heat; simmer, uncovered, 5 minutes.
5 Combine pasta in large bowl with sliced sausage, vegetable mixture and half of the mozzarella.
6 Place in 2.5-litre (10 cup) shallow baking dish; sprinkle with combined remaining cheeses. Bake, uncovered, about 25 minutes or until browned lightly.

prep + cook time 45 minutes **serves** 6

For toddlers, choose a small lettuce leaf; spoon chicken mixture into the leaf without adding green onion then roll into a small, tight cigar shape to be eaten by hand.

spaghetti with prawns and tomato

375g spaghetti
1 tablespoon olive oil
1 medium red onion (170g), chopped finely
2 cloves garlic, crushed
2 tablespoons tomato paste
700g bottled tomato pasta sauce
600g uncooked medium king prawns, shelled, deveined
½ cup (60g) seeded black olives
½ teaspoon dried chilli flakes
30g baby rocket leaves

This recipe is best made as close to serving as possible as prawns toughen on reheating.

1 Cook pasta in large saucepan of boiling water, until tender; drain. Coarsely chop some of the pasta for toddler.

2 Meanwhile, heat oil in large saucepan; cook onion and garlic, stirring, until onion softens. Add paste; cook, stirring, 1 minute. Add sauce and prawns; bring to the boil. Reduce heat; simmer, uncovered, about 3 minutes or until prawns are cooked through. Coarsely chop a prawn.

3 Combine toddler's pasta, some of the sauce and chopped prawn in a small bowl.

4 Add olives and chilli to remaining sauce, season to taste; cook, stirring, until heated through. Add remaining pasta; stir to coat in sauce. Divide into serving bowls; sprinkle with rocket.

prep + cook time 30 minutes **serves** 4

honeyed chicken drumsticks

8 chicken drumsticks (1kg)
1 tablespoon honey
¼ cup (60ml) japanese soy sauce
1 teaspoon ground cinnamon
1 tablespoon peanut oil
2 cloves garlic, crushed
2 tablespoons sweet chilli sauce
2 teaspoons finely chopped fresh coriander root and stem mixture
3cm piece fresh ginger (15g), grated
1 tablespoon dry sherry
1 teaspoon sesame seeds
1 cup (200g) jasmine rice

Serve chicken sprinkled with fresh coriander leaves, if you like. The chicken marinade mixture can be frozen for up to 2 months, thaw in the fridge overnight.
Honey may contain harmful bacteria and is not recommended for children under one year old.

1 Slash chicken several times through thickest parts of drumsticks.
2 Combine honey, soy, cinnamon, oil and garlic in large bowl. Combine 2 tablespoons of the honey mixture with one drumstick in a small bowl for the toddler. Cover; refrigerate 3 hours or overnight.
3 Add remaining chicken, sweet chilli sauce, coriander, ginger and sherry to large bowl. Cover; refrigerate 3 hours or overnight.
4 Preheat oven to 220°C/200°C fan-forced.
5 Place all chicken on oiled wire rack over large baking dish; pour excess marinades over chicken, sprinkle with seeds. Roast, uncovered, about 35 minutes or until chicken is cooked through.
6 Meanwhile, cook rice following packet instructions.
7 Remove flesh from toddler's drumstick, chop meat coarsely; serve with a little of the cooked rice.
8 Season remaining chicken and rice to taste before serving.

prep + cook time 45 minutes (+ refrigeration) **serves** 4

Omit the green onions from the stir-fry if you like. Cut toddler portion of beef into small pieces to serve.

macaroni cheese with spinach and bacon

375g elbow macaroni
300g spinach, trimmed
1 medium brown onion (150g), chopped finely
4 rindless bacon rashers (260g), chopped finely
50g butter
⅓ cup (50g) plain flour
1 litre (4 cups) hot milk
1½ cups (180g) coarsely grated cheddar cheese
½ cup (35g) stale breadcrumbs

1 Preheat oven to 200°C/180°C fan-forced.
2 Cook pasta in large saucepan of boiling water, uncovered, until just tender; drain.
3 Meanwhile, steam or microwave spinach until wilted; drain. Rinse under cold water; drain. Squeeze as much liquid as possible from spinach; chop coarsely.
4 Cook onion and bacon, stirring, in medium saucepan until onion softens. Transfer to large bowl.
5 Melt butter in same pan, add flour; cook, stirring, until mixture thickens and bubbles. Gradually add milk; stir until mixture boils and thickens. Remove from heat; stir in cheese.
6 Combine pasta, spinach and cheese sauce in bowl with onion mixture. Pour into greased shallow 2.5-litre (10 cup) flameproof casserole dish; top with breadcrumbs.
7 Cook, uncovered, in oven about 30 minutes. Place dish under preheated grill to brown lightly.

prep + cook time 50 minutes **serves** 6

stir-fried beef with hokkien noodles

2 tablespoons peanut oil
2 eggs, beaten lightly
400g thin hokkien noodles
2 cloves garlic, crushed
600g beef rump steak, sliced thinly
¼ cup (60ml) kecap manis
1 tablespoon fish sauce
1 tablespoon oyster sauce
1½ cups (120g) bean sprouts
100g enoki mushrooms, trimmed
150g oyster mushrooms, chopped coarsely
4 green onions, sliced thickly

1 Heat half of the oil in wok; cook egg over medium heat, swirling wok to make a thin omelette. Transfer to board; when cool, roll into cigar shape, slice thinly.
2 Place noodles in medium heatproof bowl; cover with boiling water, separate with fork, drain.
3 Heat remaining oil in same wok; stir-fry garlic and beef, in batches, until beef is browned. Return beef mixture to wok with noodles, sauces, sprouts, mushrooms and onion; stir-fry until heated through. Remove from heat; add sliced omelette, toss gently to combine.

prep + cook time 30 minutes **serves** 4

ricotta and spinach pasta bake

32 large pasta shells (280g)
500g spinach, trimmed
600g low-fat ricotta cheese
2 tablespoons finely chopped fresh flat-leaf parsley
1 tablespoon finely chopped fresh mint
700g bottled tomato pasta sauce
½ cup (125ml) chicken stock
2 tablespoons finely grated parmesan cheese

Serve with a green salad and crusty bread, if you like. This recipe can be prepared 3 hours ahead – keep covered in the fridge ready for baking.

1 Cook pasta in large saucepan of boiling water, 3 minutes; drain. Cool 10 minutes.
2 Preheat oven to 180°C/160°C fan-forced.
3 Boil, steam or microwave spinach until wilted; drain. Chop spinach finely; squeeze out excess liquid.
4 Combine spinach in large bowl with ricotta and herbs; spoon mixture into pasta shells.
5 Combine sauce and stock in oiled shallow 2-litre (8-cup) ovenproof dish. Place pasta shells in dish; sprinkle with parmesan. Bake, covered, about 50 minutes or until pasta is tender. Bake, uncovered, 10 minutes or until browned lightly. Remove from oven; stand 10 minutes.
6 Serve toddler two or three pasta shells; drizzle with a little of the sauce in a small bowl.
7 Divide remaining pasta shells and sauce into serving bowls; season to taste.

prep + cook time 1 hour 20 minutes **serves** 4

vegetable and chickpea fritters

1½ cup (225g) chickpea (besan) flour
1 large zucchini (150g), grated coarsely
1 large brown onion (200g), grated coarsely
1 large carrot (180g), grated coarsely
¾ cup (120g) frozen peas and corn mix
1 clove garlic, crushed
1 teaspoon ground cumin
1 teaspoon garam marsala
½ teaspoon baking powder
¼ cup (60ml) water
¼ cup coarsely chopped fresh coriander
vegetable oil for shallow frying
¾ cup (210g) yogurt

A green salad would go well with these fritters. Your hand is the best "implement" for mixing the fritter ingredients together. This is a last minute recipe, it's not suitable to freeze at any stage.

1 Combine flour, vegetables, garlic, spices, baking powder and the water in medium bowl.
2 Remove some of the vegetable mixture for toddler; shape into two or three fritters.
3 Mix coriander into remaining vegetable mixture. Shape mixture into 16 fritters.
4 Shallow-fry fritters, in batches, until browned and cooked through. Drain fritters on absorbent paper.
5 Place toddler's fritters, topped with a little of the yogurt in a small bowl.
6 Season remaining fritters to taste; serve with yogurt or dipping sauce.

prep + cook time 25 minutes **serves** 4

pear and soy smoothie

Blend or process 2 medium peeled, cored and coarsely chopped pears, 2 cups soy milk and 1 tablespoon honey until smooth.

prep time 5 minutes
makes 1 litre (4 cups)
Honey may contain harmful bacteria and is not recommended for children under one year old.

buttermilk fruit smoothie

Blend or process 1 small peeled, cored and coarsely chopped pear, 1 small coarsely chopped banana, 2 teaspoons honey, ½ cup chilled buttermilk and ½ cup chilled apple juice until smooth. Pour into glass; serve with ice.

prep time 5 minutes
makes 1 cup (250ml)
Freeze unpeeled bananas then use them straight from the freezer for an ice-creamy texture.
Honey may contain harmful bacteria and is not recommended for children under one year old.

strawberry and soy milk smoothie

Blend or process 5 hulled and halved strawberries, ½ cup chilled strawberry soy milk and ½ cup strawberry soy ice-cream until smooth. Pour into glass; serve immediately.

prep time 5 minutes
makes 1 cup (250ml)

brekky berry smoothie

Blend or process ½ cup frozen mixed berries, ½ cup chilled low-fat milk, ¼ cup low-fat vanilla yogurt and 1 Weet-Bix until smooth. Pour into glass; serve immediately.

prep time 5 minutes
makes 1 cup (250ml)

almond and berry smoothie

Blend or process 1 cup chilled water and ½ cup roasted slivered almonds until smooth. Strain mixture into small jug; discard solids. Return almond milk to blender with 3 drops vanilla extract, ⅓ cup frozen raspberries and ¾ cup reduced-fat frozen raspberry yogurt; blend until smooth. Pour into glass; serve immediately.

prep time 5 minutes
makes 1 cup (250ml)

creamy chicken crêpes

1 tablespoon finely chopped fresh chervil
2 green onions, chopped finely
50g butter
150g button mushrooms, sliced thinly
2 cloves garlic, crushed
¼ cup (60ml) dry white wine
¼ cup (35g) plain flour
3 cups (750ml) hot milk
2 cups (320g) shredded cooked chicken

crêpe batter
¾ cup (110g) plain flour
1½ cups (375ml) milk
1 egg

Serve with salad for the family and cherry tomatoes for the toddler, if you like. We used the meat from half a barbecued chicken in this recipe. Crêpes can be made and frozen, layered with freezer-friendly plastic wrap, for 2 months. Thaw crêpes in the fridge overnight. Warm crêpes, in the oven, wrapped in foil, in a slow oven for about 10 minutes. Chicken filling (without the mushroom mixture) can be made a day ahead; keep covered in the fridge. Reheat in the microwave oven, or in a saucepan over a low heat before adding the mushroom mixture.

1 Make crêpe batter.
2 Heat oiled 24cm heavy-based frying pan; pour 2 tablespoons batter into pan, tilting pan to coat base. Cook over low heat until browned lightly; loosen crêpe around edge with spatula. Turn crêpe; brown other side. Remove crêpe from pan; cover to keep warm for toddler.
3 Stir chervil and half the onion into remaining crêpe batter. Pour ¼ cup batter into pan, tilting pan to coat base. Cook over low heat until browned lightly, loosen around edge with spatula. Turn crêpe; brown other side. Remove crêpe from pan; cover to keep warm. Repeat with remaining batter to make eight herb crêpes.
4 Melt 20g of the butter in same pan; cook mushrooms and garlic, stirring, until mushrooms are tender. Add wine; bring to the boil. Boil until liquid has evaporated.
5 Meanwhile, melt remaining butter in medium saucepan. Add flour; cook, stirring, until mixture bubbles and thickens. Gradually add milk; cook, stirring, until mixture boils and thickens. Add chicken and remaining onion; stir until hot.
6 Remove a little of the chicken mixture for toddler; spread over half of toddler's crêpe, fold crêpe into quarters.
7 Stir mushroom mixture into remaining chicken mixture, season to taste; divide mixture over herb crêpes. Fold crêpes into quarters.

crêpe batter Whisk ingredients in medium bowl until smooth; strain mixture into large jug, stand 30 minutes.

prep + cook time 1 hour (+ standing) **serves** 4

pork cabbage rolls

1 small savoy cabbage (1.2kg)
400g pork mince
¾ cup (115g) cooked white long-grain rice
¼ cup (40g) dried currants
1 medium tomato (150g), seeded, chopped finely
1 clove garlic, crushed
1 cup (250ml) chicken stock
400g can diced tomatoes
2 sprigs fresh thyme

Use the rest of the cabbage for another meal, it will keep in the fridge for about 2 days. Cabbage rolls are best made just before serving.

1 Remove eight leaves from cabbage. Drop leaves, one or two at a time, into large saucepan of boiling water. Boil leaves for about 1 minute or until soft and pliable; drain. Trim and discard the hard centre ribs from each leaf; pat leaves dry with absorbent paper.
2 Combine mince, rice, currants, tomato and garlic in medium bowl.
3 Place ¼ cup mince mixture in centre of each cabbage leaf; fold in sides, roll to enclose filling.
4 Preheat oven to 200°C/180°C fan-forced.
5 Place rolls, seam-side down, in single layer, in medium baking dish. Combine stock, undrained tomatoes and thyme in large jug; pour mixture over rolls. Cook, covered, about 40 minutes or until rolls are cooked through. Discard thyme sprigs.
6 Serve toddler a small piece of cabbage roll with a little of the sauce.
7 Season remaining sauce to taste; serve with remaining pork and cabbage rolls.

prep + cook time 1 hour 30 minutes **serves** 4

zucchini, pea and mint risotto

1 litre (4 cups) chicken stock
2 cups (500ml) water
40g butter
2 large zucchini (300g), halved, sliced thinly
1 clove garlic, crushed
1 small brown onion (80g), chopped finely
2 cups (400g) arborio rice
2 cups (240g) frozen peas, thawed
⅓ cup (25g) coarsely grated parmesan cheese
1 tablespoon finely chopped fresh mint

1 Combine stock and the water in medium saucepan; bring to the boil. Reduce heat; simmer, covered.

2 Meanwhile, melt butter in large saucepan; cook zucchini and garlic, stirring, until zucchini just softens. Remove from pan.

3 Cook onion in same pan, stirring, until softened. Add rice; stir to coat rice in onion mixture. Stir in 1 cup of the simmering stock mixture; cook, stirring, over low heat until liquid is absorbed. Continue adding stock mixture, in 1-cup batches, stirring, until liquid is absorbed after each addition. Total cooking time should be about 35 minutes or until rice is just tender.

4 Gently stir zucchini mixture and peas into risotto; cook, uncovered, until peas are tender. Remove from heat; stir in cheese and mint.

prep + cook time 50 minutes **serves** 4

corn and bacon fritters

4 rindless bacon rashers (260g), chopped finely
2 cups (320g) fresh corn kernels
2 green onions, chopped finely
⅔ cup (100g) plain flour
½ teaspoon bicarbonate of soda
⅔ cup (160ml) buttermilk
2 eggs
125g can creamed corn
½ cup (125ml) sweet chilli sauce

1 Cook bacon in large non-stick frying pan until crisp. Add corn kernels and onion; cook, stirring, 2 minutes. Remove from heat.

2 Sift flour and soda into medium bowl. Make well in centre of flour mixture; gradually whisk in combined milk and eggs, whisking until batter is smooth. Stir in bacon mixture and creamed corn.

3 Pour ¼ cup batter into same heated oiled frying pan; using spatula, spread batter into round shape. Cook, two at a time, about 2 minutes each side or until fritter is browned lightly and cooked through. Remove fritters from pan; cover to keep warm. Repeat process with remaining batter.

4 Divide fritters among serving plates; serve with sweet chilli sauce.

prep + cook time 35 minutes **serves** 4

Serve your toddler a small corn and bacon fritter with tomato sauce rather than sweet chilli sauce. You need 2 fresh corn cobs for this recipe.

fish pot pies

1 cup (250ml) fish stock
⅔ cup (160ml) water
300g salmon fillets, cut into 2cm pieces
300g firm white fish fillets, cut into 2cm pieces
2 large potatoes (600g), chopped coarsely
1 small kumara (250g), chopped coarsely
2 tablespoons milk
40g butter
2 tablespoons plain flour
1 tablespoon finely chopped fresh flat-leaf parsley
½ cup (60g) coarsely grated cheddar cheese

The pies can be prepared several hours ahead, and instead of browning them under the grill, heat and brown them in the oven at 180°C/160°C fan-forced for about 30 minutes. The pies are not suitable to freeze.

1 Place stock and the water in medium saucepan; bring to the boil. Add fish, reduce heat; simmer gently, about 2 minutes or until cooked through. Remove fish from pan; place a few pieces each of salmon and white fish in 1 cup (250ml) shallow ovenproof dish for toddler, then divide remaining fish into three 2-cup (500ml) shallow ovenproof dishes. Strain stock mixture into medium jug; discard solids.
2 Boil, steam or microwave vegetables until tender; drain. Push vegetables through sieve into large bowl; stir in milk and half the butter until smooth. Cover to keep warm.
3 Preheat grill.
4 Melt remaining butter in small saucepan; add flour, cook, stirring, about 2 minutes or until mixture bubbles and thickens. Gradually stir in reserved stock mixture; cook, stirring, until sauce boils and thickens. Stir in parsley.
5 Pour a little of the sauce over toddler's fish; top with some of the vegetable mixture.
6 Pour remaining sauce over fish in large dishes, top with remaining vegetable mixture; season to taste.
7 Sprinkle dishes with cheese. Place dishes on oven tray; grill until browned lightly.

prep + cook time 50 minutes **serves** 4

spiced moroccan fish with couscous

1 cup (200g) couscous
1 cup (250ml) boiling water
20g butter, chopped coarsely
⅔ cup (50g) flaked almonds, roasted
2 tablespoons dried currants
⅓ cup coarsely chopped fresh mint
600g white fish fillet
3 teaspoons moroccan seasoning

lemon dressing
2 tablespoons olive oil
2 tablespoons lemon juice
2 teaspoons finely grated lemon rind
2 teaspoons finely chopped preserved lemon

Serve with yogurt, if you like. We used blue-eye fillets in this recipe, but any white fish fillet will be fine. Moroccan seasoning is available in the dried herbs and spices section of most supermarkets. You might want to leave the nuts out of the couscous or you might want to chop them – depending on the age of your toddler. We used a mild moroccan seasoning, if you're in doubt about using this for your toddler, don't rub it onto the toddler's fish.
This is a last minute recipe and is not suitable to freeze or microwave.

1 Combine couscous with the water in medium heatproof bowl, cover; stand 5 minutes or until liquid is absorbed, fluffing with fork occasionally. Stir in butter. Stand 10 minutes. Stir in nuts and currants; reserve some of the couscous mixture for toddler. Add mint to remaining couscous mixture; season to taste.
2 Meanwhile, make lemon dressing.
3 Cut fish into four large fillets for adults and a smaller fillet for toddler. Rub seasoning all over fish. Cook fish in heated oiled large frying pan.
4 Place toddler's couscous on serving plate. Flake toddler's fish over couscous; drizzle with toddler's lemon dressing.
5 Divide remaining couscous onto serving plates; top with remaining fish fillets and lemon dressing.
lemon dressing Place oil and juice in screw-top jar; shake well. Reserve a little of the dressing for toddler. Add rind and preserved lemon to remaining dressing; shake well.

prep + cook time 30 minutes (+ standing) **serves** 4

Give your toddler one mashed or chopped fish burger with a little of the carrot and lettuce.

If you're having the pasta, cut the fettuccine into lengths your toddler can manage easily.

fish and salad burgers

1 large potato (300g), chopped coarsely
1 tablespoon vegetable oil
1 medium brown onion (150g), chopped finely
1 clove garlic, crushed
415g can pink salmon, drained
2 teaspoons finely grated lemon rind
1 tablespoon finely chopped fresh chives
1 egg
¼ cup (35g) plain flour
1 egg, beaten lightly, extra
1 cup (70g) stale breadcrumbs
vegetable oil, extra, for shallow-frying
4 hot dog rolls
¼ cup (75g) tartare sauce
1 medium carrot (120g), grated coarsely
½ butter lettuce (100g), shredded coarsely

1 Boil, steam or microwave potato until tender; drain. Mash in medium bowl.
2 Meanwhile, heat oil in medium frying pan; cook onion and garlic, stirring, until onion softens.
3 Discard any bones from salmon; flake into bowl with potato. Add onion mixture, rind, chives and egg; use hand to combine. Roll rounded tablespoons of burger mixture into balls; flatten into slightly oval-shaped burgers (you will have 16 burgers).
4 Coat burgers with flour; shake away excess. Dip into extra egg then breadcrumbs. Cover; refrigerate 1 hour.
5 Heat oil in large frying pan; shallow-fry burgers, in batches, until cooked through. Drain on absorbent paper.
6 Halve rolls; spread sauce over cut sides, sandwich burgers, carrot and lettuce between roll halves.

prep + cook time 40 minutes (+ refrigeration) **serves** 4

fettuccine with tuna, tomato and eggplant

375g tri-colour fettuccine
1 tablespoon finely grated lemon rind
½ cup coarsely chopped fresh flat-leaf parsley
1 tablespoon olive oil
6 large egg tomatoes (540g), chopped coarsely
280g jar char-grilled eggplant, drained, chopped coarsely
425g can tuna in springwater, drained, flaked

1 Cook pasta in large saucepan of boiling water, uncovered, until just tender; drain. Combine in large bowl with rind, parsley and oil.
2 Meanwhile, cook tomato, uncovered, in oiled large frying pan until just softened. Add eggplant and tuna; cook, uncovered, until heated through.
3 Add tomato mixture to pasta mixture; toss gently to combine.

prep + cook time 20 minutes **serves** 4

meatballs napolitana

500g pork and veal mince
1 egg
½ cup (50g) packaged breadcrumbs
¼ cup (20g) finely grated parmesan cheese
¼ cup finely chopped fresh flat-leaf parsley
1 tablespoon olive oil
1 small brown onion (80g), chopped finely
1 clove garlic, crushed
700g bottled tomato pasta sauce
½ cup (60g) frozen peas
¼ cup coarsely chopped fresh basil
½ cup (60g) seeded green olives
¼ teaspoon dried chilli flakes

garlic parmesan toasts

1 small french bread stick (150g), sliced thickly
1 clove garlic, halved
⅓ cup (25g) finely grated parmesan cheese

1 Combine mince, egg, breadcrumbs, cheese and parsley in medium bowl. Roll level tablespoons of mince mixture into balls.
2 Heat half the oil in large frying pan; cook meatballs until browned and cooked through. Remove meatballs from pan.
3 Heat remaining oil in same pan; cook onion and garlic, stirring, until onion softens. Add sauce; bring to the boil. Add meatballs, reduce heat; simmer, uncovered, about 10 minutes or until sauce thickens slightly.
4 Meanwhile, make garlic parmesan toasts.
5 Add peas and basil to meatball mixture; simmer, uncovered, until peas are tender.
6 Serve toddler some of the meatball and sauce mixture with a garlic parmesan toast.
7 Add olives and chilli to remaining meatball mixture, season to taste; stir until heated through. Serve with remaining garlic parmesan toasts.

garlic parmesan toasts Preheat grill. Toast bread slices one side, rub with cut-sides of garlic. Turn toasts, sprinkle with cheese; grill until cheese melts.

---

prep + cook time 1 hour **serves** 4

cheesy pumpkin polenta fingers

500g piece pumpkin, chopped coarsely
2 tablespoons olive oil
3 cups (750ml) water
¾ cup (125g) polenta
¼ cup (20g) finely grated parmesan cheese
20g baby rocket leaves

ratatouille
1 small eggplant (230g)
2 medium zucchini (240g)
1 medium red capsicum (200g)
2 tablespoons olive oil
½ small red onion (50g), chopped coarsely
2 cloves garlic, crushed
400g can crushed tomatoes
½ cup (130g) bottled tomato pasta sauce
½ cup (125ml) water
¼ cup loosely packed fresh small basil leaves

Add a little sugar to the ratatouille to reduce any acid taste, if you like. It's not essential to peel the eggplant or zucchini, but if by peeling them the toddler will eat these vegies, then it's worth the effort. If you want to reduce or eliminate the oil, the ratatouille can be cooked in the oven. Combine all the ingredients in an ovenproof dish and bake at 180°C/160°C fan-forced for about 30 minutes.

1 Preheat oven to 220°C/200°C fan-forced. Grease deep 20cm-square cake pan.
2 Toss pumpkin with half the oil in medium shallow baking dish; roast, in single layer, 30 minutes.
3 Place the water in medium saucepan; bring to the boil. Gradually add polenta to water, stirring constantly, reduce heat. Simmer, stirring, about 10 minutes or until polenta thickens. Remove from heat, stir in cheese, rocket and pumpkin; spread into pan, cool 10 minutes. Cover; refrigerate about 1 hour or until firm.
4 Meanwhile, make ratatouille.
5 Turn polenta onto board; trim edges. Cut into quarters; cut each quarter into three slices. Heat remaining oil in large frying pan; cook polenta, until browned all over. Reserve a slice of polenta for toddler; cut into bite-sized pieces.
6 Place toddler's polenta on serving plate; top with some ratatouille.
7 Divide remaining polenta slices onto serving plates; top with remaining ratatouille, serve with rocket.

ratatouille Peel eggplant; randomly peel zucchini. Chop eggplant, zucchini and capsicum into 1cm pieces. Heat half the oil in large frying pan; cook eggplant and zucchini, stirring, until browned all over. Remove from pan. Heat remaining oil in same pan; cook capsicum, onion and garlic, stirring, until onion softens. Add undrained tomatoes, sauce, the water and eggplant mixture; bring to the boil. Reduce heat, simmer, uncovered, about 10 minutes or until vegetables are tender. Remove from heat; stir in basil. Reserve 2 cups for the ratatouille pasta salad recipe (page 131).

prep + cook time 1 hour 10 minutes (+ refrigeration) **serves** 4

spaghetti bolognese

1 tablespoon olive oil
1 medium brown onion (150g), chopped finely
2 cloves garlic, crushed
1 medium carrot (120g), chopped finely
1 stalk celery (150g), trimmed, chopped finely
500g lean beef mince
2 x 400g cans crushed tomatoes
⅓ cup (95g) tomato paste
2 tablespoons finely chopped fresh basil
375g spaghetti
¼ cup (20g) finely grated parmesan cheese

1 Heat oil in large saucepan; cook onion, garlic, carrot and celery, stirring, until vegetables soften. Add mince; cook, stirring, about 5 minutes or until mince is browned. Add undrained tomatoes and paste; bring to the boil. Reduce heat; simmer, uncovered, about 15 minutes or until sauce thickens. Add basil; simmer, uncovered, 5 minutes. Reserve 2 cups of mixture for potato smash with bolognese and eggplant (page 141).
2 Meanwhile, cook pasta in large saucepan boiling water until tender; drain. Reserve a little of the pasta for toddler; chop pasta coarsely.
3 Combine toddler's pasta and some of the bolognese sauce in small bowl.
4 Divide remaining pasta into serving bowls. Season remaining bolognese sauce to taste, spoon over pasta; sprinkle with cheese.

prep + cook time 35 minutes **serves** 4

bolognese and spinach potato pie

1 tablespoon olive oil
1 small brown onion (80g), chopped finely
1 clove garlic, crushed
250g beef mince
1 small carrot (70g), grated coarsely
1 small red capsicum (150g), chopped finely
50g mushrooms, sliced thinly
2 tablespoons tomato paste
¼ cup (60ml) dry red wine
425g can crushed tomatoes
300g spinach, trimmed, chopped coarsely
5 medium potatoes (1.2kg)
40g unsalted butter
2 cloves garlic, crushed
2 eggs, beaten lightly
½ cup (50g) coarsely grated mozzarella cheese

1 Heat oil in large saucepan; cook onion and garlic, stirring, until onion softens. Add beef, carrot, capsicum and mushrooms; cook, stirring, until beef changes colour.
2 Add paste, wine and undrained tomatoes; bring to the boil. Reduce heat; simmer, uncovered, about 30 minutes or until sauce thickens. Stir spinach into bolognese sauce.
3 Meanwhile, preheat oven to 180°C/160°C fan-forced.
4 Boil, steam or microwave potatoes until tender; drain. Mash potatoes in large bowl with butter, garlic and egg until smooth.
5 Spread half of the potato mixture over base and sides of 1.5-litre (6 cup) pie dish; spread bolognese sauce over potato then gently spread remaining potato mixture over bolognese sauce. Sprinkle with cheese.
6 Cook pie, uncovered, in oven 30 minutes or until browned lightly.

prep + cook time 1 hour 15 minutes **serves** 6

potato and bacon soup

40g butter
1 medium brown onion (150g), chopped finely
1 clove garlic, crushed
4 rindless bacon rashers (260g), chopped coarsely
¼ cup (35g) plain flour
2 cups (500ml) chicken stock
2 cups (500ml) milk
3 medium potatoes (600g), chopped coarsely
½ cup (125ml) cream
2 tablespoons finely chopped fresh chives

1 Heat butter in large saucepan; cook onion, garlic and bacon, stirring, until onion softens.
2 Add flour; cook, stirring, until mixture thickens and bubbles. Gradually add stock and milk; stir until mixture boils and thickens.
3 Stir in potato; return to the boil. Reduce heat; simmer, covered, about 20 minutes or until potato softens. Stir in cream and chives.

prep + cook time 40 minutes **serves** 4

Making a potato pie is the perfect way to use any leftover bolognese sauce (see previous page) you may have from another meal. You will need 3 cups of sauce for this recipe.

honey and soy drumsticks with easy fried rice

- ⅓ cup (80ml) soy sauce
- ¼ cup (90g) honey
- 8 chicken drumsticks (1.2kg)
- 2 teaspoons vegetable oil
- 2 eggs, beaten lightly
- 4 rindless bacon rashers (260g), chopped coarsely
- 1 medium brown onion (150g), chopped finely
- 1 stalk celery (150g), trimmed, chopped finely
- 3 cups (600g) cooked white long-grain rice
- ½ cup (80g) frozen corn kernels, thawed
- ½ cup (60g) frozen peas, thawed
- 2 tablespoons soy sauce, extra
- 2 green onions, chopped finely

You need to cook 1½ cups (300g) white long-grain rice the day before for this recipe. Remove skin from chicken and cut the meat off the bone for your toddler. Honey may contain harmful bacteria and is not recommended for children under one year old.

1 Combine soy and honey in large bowl with chicken. Cover; refrigerate 3 hours or overnight.
2 Preheat oven to 180°C/160°C fan-forced.
3 Place undrained chicken, in single layer, in large shallow baking dish; cook, uncovered, in oven about 40 minutes or until cooked through, turning occasionally.
4 Meanwhile, heat ½ teaspoon of the oil in wok; cook half of the egg mixture over medium heat, swirling wok to make a thin omelette. Transfer to board; when cool enough to handle, roll into cigar shape, slice thinly. Repeat with another ½ teaspoon of the oil and remaining egg.
5 Heat remaining oil in same wok; stir-fry bacon, brown onion and celery until onion softens. Add rice, corn, peas and extra soy; stir-fry until heated through.
6 Sprinkle green onion over fried rice before serving with chicken.

prep + cook time 1 hour (+ refrigeration) **serves** 4

Pasta is at its best cooked and eaten straight away, however, you can freeze small, chopped up portions for toddlers. The same goes for any leftover ratatouille. Pasta and ratatouille thaw well in the microwave.

Purée one meatball with a toddler-size portion of the soup for the child's serving.

ratatouille pasta salad

375g rigatoni pasta
½ rindless bacon rasher (30g), chopped coarsely
1 chorizo sausage (170g), sliced thinly
2 cups (400g) reserved ratatouille (see page 123)
⅓ cup (25g) shaved parmesan cheese
⅓ cup (50g) semi-dried tomatoes in oil, drained, chopped coarsely
¼ cup firmly packed fresh small basil leaves

You could substitute the bacon and chorizo with ham and mild salami if you prefer.

1 Cook pasta in large saucepan boiling water until tender. Reserve ¼ cup of the cooking liquid; drain pasta. Coarsely chop a little of the cooked pasta for toddler.
2 Meanwhile, cook bacon and chorizo, separately, in medium heated frying pan, stirring, until crisp. Drain separately on absorbent paper.
3 Combine toddler's pasta, all the bacon, 1 tablespoon reserved cooking liquid and some ratatouille in small bowl.
4 Combine remaining pasta, ratatouille and reserved cooking liquid with chorizo, cheese, tomato and basil in large bowl, season to taste; divide into serving bowls.

prep + cook time 25 minutes **serves** 4

minestrone with meatballs

400g pork mince
1 teaspoon sweet paprika
1 egg, beaten lightly
1 medium brown onion (150g), chopped finely
¼ cup (70g) tomato paste
2 tablespoons olive oil
2 cloves garlic, crushed
2 medium carrots (240g), diced into 1cm pieces
1 stalk celery (150g), trimmed, diced into 1cm pieces
2 x 425g cans diced tomatoes
2 cups (500ml) chicken stock
2 cups (500ml) water
2 large zucchini (300g), diced into 1cm pieces
400g can borlotti beans, rinsed, drained
½ cup (110g) risoni

1 Combine mince, paprika, egg, half of the onion and 1 tablespoon of the tomato paste in medium bowl. Roll level tablespoons of mixture into balls.
2 Heat oil in large saucepan; cook meatballs, in batches, until browned.
3 Cook garlic and remaining onion in same pan, stirring, until onion softens. Add carrot and celery; cook, stirring, until vegetables are just tender. Add remaining paste; cook, stirring, 1 minute. Add undrained tomatoes, stock and the water; bring to the boil.
4 Add zucchini, beans, risoni and meatballs; return to the boil. Reduce heat; simmer, covered, about 15 minutes or until meatballs are cooked through.

prep + cook time 1 hour 15 minutes **serves** 4

tuna potato salad

2 medium potatoes (400g), unpeeled, chopped coarsely
100g green beans, trimmed, halved crossways
200g tuna steak
1 tablespoon drained canned tuna in springwater
250g grape tomatoes, halved
80g baby spinach leaves
⅓ cup (40g) seeded black olives

lemon dressing

⅓ cup (80ml) lemon juice
2 tablespoons olive oil
1 clove garlic, crushed
¼ teaspoon ground cumin

1 Boil, steam or microwave potato and beans, separately, until tender; drain. Rinse beans under cold water; drain.
2 Meanwhile, make lemon dressing.
3 Cook tuna steak on heated oiled grill plate (or grill or barbecue) until cooked as desired. Cover tuna, stand 5 minutes; slice thinly.
4 Combine some of the canned tuna, tomato, spinach, potato, beans and the toddler's dressing in small bowl.
5 Divide remaining ingredients onto serving plates; top with sliced tuna, season to taste; drizzle with remaining lemon dressing.
lemon dressing Place juice and oil in screw-top jar; shake well. Reserve a little of the dressing for toddler's salad. Add garlic and cumin to remaining dressing, season to taste; shake until combined.

prep + cook time 30 minutes serves 4

crumbed fish with honey and soy baked vegetables

500g firm white fish fillets
¼ cup (35g) plain flour
2 eggs, beaten lightly
1 tablespoon finely chopped fresh flat-leaf parsley
1½ cups (110g) stale breadcrumbs
400g small potatoes, quartered
400g pumpkin, chopped coarsely
2 medium carrots (240g), chopped coarsely
2 tablespoons honey
1 tablespoon soy sauce
1 tablespoon vegetable oil
olive oil, for shallow-frying

Honey may contain harmful bacteria and is not recommended for children under one year old.

1 Preheat oven to 220°C/200°C fan-forced.
2 Halve fish fillets lengthways. Coat fish pieces, one at a time, in flour, then egg, then in combined parsley and breadcrumbs. Place in single layer on tray, cover; refrigerate 15 minutes.
3 Meanwhile, boil, steam or microwave potato, pumpkin and carrot, separately, until just tender; drain.
4 Combine vegetables with honey, soy and vegetable oil in large shallow baking dish; roast, uncovered, about 30 minutes or until vegetables are browned.
5 Heat olive oil in large deep frying pan; shallow-fry fish, in batches, until browned and cooked through. Drain on absorbent paper. Serve fish with vegetables.

prep + cook time 1 hour (+ refrigeration) **serves** 4

chicken and vegetable risotto

3 cups (750ml) chicken stock
2 cups (500ml) water
1 tablespoon olive oil
300g chicken breast fillets, chopped coarsely
1 medium brown onion (150g), chopped finely
1 clove garlic, crushed
1½ cups (300g) arborio rice
1 cup (120g) frozen peas
2 teaspoons finely grated lemon rind
2 tablespoons finely chopped fresh mint
170g asparagus, trimmed, chopped coarsely

1 Bring stock and the water to the boil in medium saucepan. Reduce heat; simmer, covered.
2 Meanwhile, heat half the oil in large saucepan; cook chicken, in batches, until browned.
3 Heat remaining oil in same pan; cook onion and garlic, stirring, until onion softens. Add rice; stir to coat rice in onion mixture. Add 1 cup simmering stock mixture; cook, stirring, over low heat, until stock is absorbed. Continue adding stock mixture in 1 cup batches, stirring until absorbed between additions. Total cooking time should be about 25 minutes or until rice is tender.
4 Add peas and rind to pan; stir until hot. Remove some risotto for toddler; serve sprinkled with a little of the mint.
5 Add chicken and asparagus to remaining risotto, season to taste; stir until chicken is heated through and asparagus is tender. Serve sprinkled with remaining mint.

prep + cook time 55 minutes **serves** 4

Save a small piece of uncrumbed fish for your child, cooking it in the oven, wrapped in oiled foil, for about the last 5 minutes of vegetable roasting time. Cut into bite-size pieces, checking there are no bones, and serve with a few tablespoons of the vegetables, mashed.

portable food

dried fruit mix

Combine ½ cup finely chopped dried pears, ½ cup finely chopped dried apricots, ⅔ cup finely chopped dried apples and ⅓ cup dried cranberries in medium bowl.

prep time 10 minutes
makes 2 cups

crudités

A perfect lunchbox snack is assorted crudités – try using cheese slices cut into different shapes using a cookie cutter, or briefly cooked carrot sticks, broccoli florets, kumara rounds or capsicum strips.

prep time 10 minutes

mixed berry yogurt

Combine ⅓ cup frozen mixed berries and ¾ cup natural or vanilla yogurt in small bowl.

prep time 5 minutes
makes about 1 cup

vegemite, cheese and lettuce sandwich

Spread one slice of white bread with ½ teaspoon vegemite; top with 1 tablespoon coarsely grated cheddar cheese, 1 tablespoon finely shredded iceberg lettuce and a second slice of white bread. Remove and discard crusts; cut sandwich into squares.

prep time 5 minutes
makes 1

banana and honey fruit loaf sandwich

Spread one slice of fruit loaf with ½ teaspoon honey; top with ½ small thinly sliced ripe banana and a second slice of fruit loaf. Remove and discard crusts; cut sandwich into fingers.

prep time 5 minutes
makes 1

Honey may contain harmful bacteria and is not recommended for children under one year old.

honey and balsamic glazed lamb shanks

8 french-trimmed lamb shanks (1.7kg)
2 cups (500ml) chicken stock
¼ cup (60ml) balsamic vinegar
¼ cup (90g) honey
2 cloves garlic, crushed
400g baby new potatoes
400g pumpkin, chopped coarsely
2 teaspoons olive oil
150g green beans, trimmed

Remove the skin from the cooked potato if necessary. Honey may contain harmful bacteria and is not recommended for children under one year old.

1 Preheat oven to 220°C/200°C fan-forced.
2 Combine lamb, stock, vinegar, honey and garlic in large flameproof dish. Bring to the boil over high heat; remove from heat, cover tightly.
3 Transfer dish to oven; cook shanks, turning once, about 2 hours or until lamb is tender.
4 Meanwhile, combine potato and pumpkin in small shallow baking dish; drizzle with oil. Roast, uncovered, with lamb, about 45 minutes.
5 Boil, steam or microwave beans until tender; drain.
6 For toddler, mash a little potato and pumpkin in a small bowl until almost smooth. Remove some meat from a lamb shank, chop coarsely; serve with vegetable mash.
7 Season remaining lamb and vegetables to taste before serving.

prep + cook time 2 hours 20 minutes **serves** 4

pork and vegetable sang choy bow

1 tablespoon peanut oil
1 small carrot (70g), chopped finely
115g baby corn, chopped finely
1 stalk celery (150g), trimmed, chopped finely
2cm piece fresh ginger (10g), grated
2 cloves garlic, crushed
700g pork mince
¼ cup (60ml) beef stock
1 baby cos lettuce, leaves separated
1 tablespoon kecap manis
2 teaspoons sambal oelek
2 tablespoons lime juice
½ cup (40g) bean sprouts
¼ cup loosely packed fresh coriander leaves

1 Heat oil in wok; stir-fry carrot, corn, celery, ginger and garlic until vegetables are tender. Add mince; stir-fry until mince browns. Add stock; bring to the boil.
2 Remove of little of the pork mixture for toddler; serve with some finely shredded lettuce.
3 Add kecap manis, sambal oelek, juice and sprouts to wok, season to taste; stir-fry until hot.
4 Divide pork mixture into remaining lettuce leaves; serve sprinkled with coriander.

prep + cook time 35 minutes **serves** 4

The cooked lamb can be removed from the bones and the meat frozen for 2 months. Thaw in the fridge overnight.

For the sang choy bow, the mince filling can be made several hours ahead; keep covered in the fridge. Stir-fry over a medium heat to reheat.

potato smash with beef and eggplant

500g baby new potatoes
1 tablespoon olive oil
1 medium eggplant (300g), peeled, chopped coarsely
2 cups (500g) bolognese sauce (see page 124)
½ cup (125ml) water
1 tablespoon finely chopped fresh flat-leaf parsley
½ teaspoon dried chilli flakes

This recipe is best made close to serving.

1 Preheat oven to 220°C/200°C fan-forced.
2 Place potatoes in small shallow baking dish; drizzle with half the oil. Roast about 40 minutes or until tender. Press potatoes with back of a fork or potato masher until skins burst.
3 Meanwhile, heat remaining oil in large saucepan; cook eggplant, stirring, until browned and tender. Remove from pan.
4 Combine bolognese sauce and the water in same pan; cook, stirring until heated through. Serve toddler some of the bolognese with a little crushed potato; sprinkle with a little of the parsley.
5 Add eggplant and chilli to remaining bolognese sauce, season to taste; cook, stirring, until heated through. Serve bolognese mixture with remaining potato; sprinkle with remaining parsley.

prep + cook time 1 hour **serves** 4

chicken schnitzel burgers

4 single chicken breast fillets (680g)
¼ cup (35g) plain flour
1 egg
1 tablespoon milk
1 cup (70g) stale breadcrumbs
¼ cup (60ml) olive oil
3 medium red onions (510g), sliced thinly
1 loaf turkish bread (430g), cut into four pieces
⅓ iceberg lettuce (200g), shredded coarsely

capsicum and caper mayonnaise

¼ cup (75g) mayonnaise
⅓ cup (65g) char-grilled red capsicum, chopped finely
1 tablespoon drained capers, rinsed, chopped coarsely

toddler tip Cut part of one of the schnitzels into finger-size pieces and serve with tomato sauce instead of the capsicum and caper mayonnaise.

1 Using meat mallet, gently pound fillets between pieces of plastic wrap until 1cm thick. Toss chicken in flour; shake away excess. Dip into combined egg and milk then breadcrumbs. Cover; refrigerate 1 hour.

2 Meanwhile, combine ingredients for capsicum and caper mayonnaise in small bowl. Cover; refrigerate until required.

3 Heat 1 tablespoon of the oil in large frying pan; cook onion, uncovered, stirring occasionally, about 15 minutes or until caramelised. Transfer to small bowl; cover to keep warm.

4 Heat remaining oil in same cleaned frying pan; cook chicken, in batches, until cooked through. Drain on absorbent paper; cover to keep warm.

5 Meanwhile, split bread pieces in half; toast cut sides of bread. Sandwich chicken, onion, mayonnaise and lettuce between bread halves.

prep + cook time 1 hour (+ refrigeration) **serves** 4

Patties are best made and cooked just before serving; they don't freeze well. Uncooked patties minus the cheese can be stacked, layered with freezer-proof plastic wrap, and frozen for 2 months.

chicken, carrot and fetta patties

700g chicken mince
1 egg
½ cup (50g) packaged breadcrumbs
1 small carrot (70g), grated coarsely
2 green onions, chopped finely
¼ cup finely chopped fresh flat-leaf parsley
100g fetta cheese, crumbled
1 tablespoon olive oil

1 Combine mince, egg, breadcrumbs, carrot, onion and parsley in large bowl.
2 Remove about ¼ cup chicken mixture for toddler; shape into three patties.
3 Add cheese to remaining chicken mixture, season to taste; mix well. Shape mixture into 16 patties.
4 Heat oil in large frying pan; cook patties until browned and cooked through.
5 Serve toddler's patties with cherry tomatoes and cucumber sticks, and/or tomato sauce.
6 Serve remaining patties with a mango or tomato chutney, a mash and a green salad.

prep + cook time 30 minutes **serves** 4

glazed meatloaf

1 trimmed corn cob (250g)
1 medium carrot (120g), grated coarsely
1 medium zucchini (120g), grated coarsely
1 baby beetroot (25g), peeled, grated coarsely
600g beef mince
1 egg
½ cup (50g) packaged breadcrumbs
2 tablespoons tomato sauce
2 tablespoons barbecue sauce

Meatloaf is good served hot, warm or cold – serve it as a meal with mash and green vegies or a salad. Cold meatloaf makes a great sandwich filling. Meatloaf doesn't freeze well.

1 Preheat oven to 200°C/180°C fan-forced. Grease 12cm x 22cm loaf pan.
2 Remove kernels from corn; combine corn, carrot, zucchini, beetroot, mince, egg and breadcrumbs in large bowl. Press mixture into pan.
3 Cover pan with foil; bake 40 minutes. Remove loaf from oven; drain excess juices from pan.
4 Turn pan upside-down onto foil- or baking-paper-lined oven tray; remove pan. Brush loaf with combined sauces; bake, uncovered, brushing occasionally with sauce mixture, about 20 minutes or until loaf is cooked through. Stand 10 minutes before slicing thickly.
5 Cut a slice of the meatloaf into fingers for toddler; serve with extra tomato sauce.
6 Season remaining meatloaf to taste; serve with mustard, horseradish or chutney.

prep + cook time 1 hour 15 minutes **serves** 4

lamb and kidney bean cassoulet

400g lamb sausages, sliced thickly
2 rindless bacon rashers (130g), chopped coarsely
1 medium brown onion (150g), chopped coarsely
2 cloves garlic, crushed
1 sprig fresh rosemary
2 bay leaves
400g can crushed tomatoes
420g can kidney beans, rinsed, drained
1 cup (250ml) chicken stock
2 cups (140g) stale breadcrumbs
⅓ cup coarsely chopped fresh flat-leaf parsley

This is a complete meal in a dish, but, it doesn't reheat or freeze well, as the breadcrumbs absorb the moisture as it stands. Packaged japanese breadcrumbs (panko) can be bought from supermarkets which stock Japanese ingredients, they're an excellent substitute for stale breadcrumbs.

1 Preheat oven to 180°C/160°C fan-forced.
2 Cook sausages in large flameproof dish over medium heat until browned all over; remove from dish. Cook bacon in same dish, stirring, until crisp; remove from dish.
3 Cook onion and garlic in same dish, stirring, until onion softens. Add rosemary, bay leaves, undrained tomatoes, beans, stock, sausages and bacon; bring to the boil. Cover; transfer to oven, bake 30 minutes. Remove from oven, remove rosemary and bay leaves; sprinkle with combined breadcrumbs and parsley. Return to oven; bake, uncovered, about 35 minutes or until liquid is nearly absorbed.
4 Serve about ½ cup cassoulet to toddler.
5 Divide remaining cassoulet into serving bowls; season to taste.

prep + cook 1 hour 30 minutes **serves** 4

parmesan schnitzels with kumara and broccoli mash

1 cup (100g) packaged breadcrumbs
½ cup (40g) finely grated parmesan cheese
¼ cup finely chopped fresh flat-leaf parsley
2 eggs
8 x 100g veal schnitzels
¼ cup (60ml) olive oil
2 medium kumara (800g), chopped coarsely
300g broccoli, chopped coarsely
20g butter

1 Combine breadcrumbs, cheese and parsley in medium shallow bowl. Whisk eggs in another medium shallow bowl. Coat schnitzels, one at a time, in egg then in breadcrumb mixture.
2 Heat half the oil in large frying pan; cook half the schnitzels until golden brown. Repeat with remaining oil and schnitzels.
3 Meanwhile, boil, steam or microwave vegetables, separately, until tender; drain. Mash vegetables with butter in medium bowl until almost smooth.
4 Cut part of a schnitzel into fingers for toddler; serve with some of the mash.
5 Divide remaining schnitzels onto serving plates, season to taste; serve with remaining mash.

prep + cook time 40 minutes **serves** 4

beef stir-fry with hokkien noodles

450g thin hokkien noodles
2 tablespoons peanut oil
700g beef rump steak, sliced thinly
1 medium red capsicum (200g), sliced thinly
100g button mushrooms, sliced thinly
3cm piece fresh ginger (15g), grated
2 cloves garlic, crushed
2 tablespoons hoisin sauce
2 tablespoons light soy sauce
4 green onions, sliced thickly

This is a last minute meal, although all the chopping can be done several hours ahead of stir-frying.

1 Place noodles in medium heatproof bowl, cover with boiling water; separate with fork, drain.
2 Heat half the oil in wok; stir-fry beef, in batches, until browned.
3 Heat remaining oil in wok; stir-fry capsicum, mushrooms, ginger and garlic until capsicum is tender.
4 Return beef to wok with noodles, sauces and onion; stir-fry until hot.
5 Coarsely chop some of the stir-fry for toddler. Divide remaining stir-fry onto serving plates.

prep + cook time 25 minutes **serves** 4

Serve schnitzels with a green salad and lemon wedges. The schnitzels can be crumbed then refrigerated for several hours ahead of cooking. The mash is best made just before serving. Make sure you don't overcook the schnitzels.

lentil and rice stew

1 cup (200g) brown lentils
1.125 litres (4½ cups) water
½ cup (100g) white long-grain rice
1 teaspoon ground allspice
4 pocket pitta breads (340g)
½ cup coarsely chopped fresh coriander

caramelised onion
1 tablespoon olive oil
2 medium brown onions (300g), sliced thinly
2 teaspoons brown sugar
1 tablespoon balsamic vinegar
⅓ cup (60ml) water

This is a hearty wintry recipe, similar to a Lebanese recipe known as mejadra (mujaddara). The lentil and rice mixture could be made ahead and frozen. Thaw in the fridge overnight, or reheat in a microwave oven. You might need to add a little more stock or water to bring the stew to the consistency you like. The onions are best cooked just before serving.

1 Combine lentils and 2½ cups of the water in medium saucepan; bring to the boil. Reduce heat; simmer, covered, about 25 minutes or until tender. Add rice, the remaining water and allspice; bring to the boil. Reduce heat; simmer, covered, stirring occasionally, about 15 minutes or until rice is tender.
2 Meanwhile, make caramelised onion.
3 Serve toddler a little of the lentil mixture with some of the pitta bread.
4 Season remaining lentil mixture to taste; stir in coriander. Serve bowls of stew topped with caramelised onion and remaining pitta.

caramelised onion Heat oil in large frying pan; cook onion, stirring, until onion softens. Add sugar, vinegar and the water; cook, stirring, about 10 minutes or until onions are caramelised.

prep + cook time 50 minutes **serves** 4

fish fingers with coleslaw

1kg white fish fillets, skin removed, chopped coarsely
2 tablespoons coarsely chopped fresh chives
2 egg whites
1¼ cups (125g) packaged breadcrumbs
2 tablespoons olive oil

coleslaw

1½ cups (120g) finely shredded red cabbage
1 cup (80g) finely shredded savoy cabbage
1 medium carrot (120g), grated coarsely
2 tablespoons coarsely chopped fresh flat-leaf parsley
1 green onion, sliced thinly
2 tablespoons mayonnaise
1 tablespoon sour cream
1 tablespoon white wine vinegar

We used ling fillets in this recipe, but any white fish fillets will do. You could serve the fish fingers with lemon wedges and oven-baked potato wedges. Fish fingers can be crumbed, placed on a tray in a single layer, covered, then refrigerated for several hours ahead of cooking. Coleslaw can be made and refrigerated up to 3 hours ahead of serving time.

1 Make coleslaw.
2 Grease 19cm x 30cm lamington pan.
3 Blend or process fish and chives until smooth. Press mixture evenly into pan, turn onto baking-paper-lined tray; cut into eight 19cm slices; cut each slice in half to make 16 fish fingers.
4 Whisk egg whites lightly in medium shallow bowl; place breadcrumbs in another medium shallow bowl. Dip fish fingers into egg whites, then in breadcrumbs to coat. Heat oil in large frying pan; cook fish fingers, in batches, until browned lightly and cooked through. Drain on absorbent paper.
5 Cut part of a fish finger into pieces for toddler; serve with a little of the coleslaw.
6 Divide remaining fish fingers and coleslaw onto serving plates; season to taste.

coleslaw Combine ingredients in large bowl.

---

prep + cook time 35 minutes **serves** 4

There was an old woman

There was an old woman
who lived in a shoe,
She had so many children she
didn't know what to do.
She gave them some broth
without any bread;
She whipped them all soundly
and put them to bed.

pizza fingers

430g loaf turkish bread
¼ cup (65g) basil pesto
⅓ cup (50g) semi-dried tomatoes in oil, drained, chopped finely
10 cherry bocconcini (150g), sliced thinly
¼ cup (70g) tomato paste
⅓ cup (90g) drained pineapple pieces, chopped coarsely
2 rindless bacon rashers (130g), sliced thinly
½ cup (60g) coarsely grated cheddar cheese
2 tablespoons small fresh basil leaves

Serve with a green salad. Toddlers and grown-ups alike will love this recipe. The fingers can be prepared several hours ahead of baking. They're not suitable to freeze

1 Preheat oven to 180°C/160°C fan-forced.
2 Cut bread into 2cm wide slices. Place slices flat on baking-paper-lined oven trays; toast about 10 minutes or until crisp.
3 Spread half the slices with pesto; top with semi-dried tomato and bocconcini. Spread remaining bread pieces with tomato paste; top with pineapple, bacon and cheddar. Bake about 12 minutes.
4 Place pizza fingers on platter; top with basil leaves.

prep + cook time 30 minutes **makes** 20

prosciutto and sage pork fillet

500g pork fillet
12 fresh sage leaves
8 slices prosciutto (90g)
1 tablespoon olive oil
800g potatoes, chopped coarsely
150g baby green beans, trimmed
¼ cup (60ml) hot milk
20g butter

The pork can be prepared several hours ahead, ready for roasting. The mash is best made just before serving. This recipe is not suitable to freeze.

1 Preheat oven to 220°C/200°C fan-forced.
2 Cut a small piece of pork from the fillet for the toddler; cut remaining pork into four equal-sized pieces. Place three sage leaves over each large piece of pork; then wrap each in two slices of prosciutto.
3 Heat oil in medium frying pan; cook all pork, until browned all over. Place pork on baking-paper-lined oven tray. Roast, in oven, about 10 minutes or until cooked as desired. Remove from oven; stand 5 minutes. Slice prosciutto-wrapped pork thickly; cut toddler's pork into bite-sized pieces.
4 Meanwhile, boil, steam or microwave potato and beans, separately, until tender; drain. Push potato through sieve into large bowl; stir in milk and butter to make a smooth mash.
5 Serve toddler's pork with a little of the potato mash and some of the beans.
6 Divide remaining mash and beans onto serving plates, top with sliced pork; season to taste.

prep + cook time 40 minutes **serves** 4

baby puddings

Wanting to give your children the best start in life doesn't mean they need to avoid sweet treats altogether. Rather, introduce your baby to sweet food by giving him healthy sweet food. Starting a child off with healthy food like fruit dishes and milk puddings will mean that he will grow up without an excessively sweet tooth. Sweet foods are indeed treats, but they don't have to be bad for your baby, or for you for that matter. Try sweetening cakes with fruit such as pineapple or mashed banana instead of refined sugars, avoid any highly processed bought cakes and biscuits, and chances are the whole family will benefit.

muesli lunchbox cookies

250g butter, softened
1¼ cups (275g) firmly packed brown sugar
1 egg
¼ cup (60ml) milk
1¼ cups (185g) plain flour
½ teaspoon bicarbonate of soda
3½ cups fruit and cereal snack mix (see recipe page 195)
2 cups (180g) rolled oats

1 Preheat oven to 180°C/160°C fan-forced. Grease oven trays; line with baking paper.
2 Beat butter and sugar in small bowl with electric mixer until light and fluffy. Beat in egg and milk until combined; transfer mixture to large bowl. Stir in sifted flour and soda, snack mix and oats until combined. Drop rounded tablespoons of mixture onto trays, about 4cm apart.
3 Bake cookies about 15 minutes. Stand cookies on trays 5 minutes; transfer to wire rack to cool.

prep + cook time 1 hour 10 minutes **makes about** 50

rhubarb, apple and pear crumble

3 stalks rhubarb, trimmed, chopped coarsely
2 medium apples (300g), peeled, chopped coarsely
1 small pear (180g), peeled, chopped coarsely
¼ cup (60ml) water
¼ cup (35g) plain flour
¼ cup (20g) rolled oats
2 tablespoons brown sugar
30g butter, chopped

1 Preheat oven to 200°C/180°C fan-forced. Grease deep 1 litre (4 cup) ovenproof dish.
2 Place rhubarb, apple, pear and water in medium saucepan; bring to the boil. Reduce heat; simmer, covered, stirring occasionally, about 10 minutes or until fruit is tender.
3 Meanwhile, combine flour, oats and sugar in small bowl; rub in butter.
4 Spoon fruit mixture into dish; sprinkle with oat mixture.
5 Bake crumble about 30 minutes or until browned lightly.

prep + cook time 45 minutes **serves** 4

The cookies will keep in an airtight container for a week, or they can be frozen for up to 2 months.

The crumbles can be made in individual dishes and frozen, before baking, for up to 2 months.

Serve crêpes dusted with icing sugar, if you like. You could use frozen ready-made crêpes, or freeze your own. The filling needs to be made on the day of serving.

Honey may contain harmful bacteria and is not recommended for children under one year old.

ricotta and honey crêpes

½ cup (75g) plain flour
1 cup (250ml) milk
1 egg
250g ricotta cheese
⅓ cup (55g) sultanas
2 teaspoons honey

1 Sift flour into small bowl; whisk in combined milk and egg until smooth. Strain batter into medium jug; stand 30 minutes.
2 Meanwhile, combine cheese, sultanas and honey in small bowl.
3 Heat a small greased heavy-based frying pan. Pour 2 tablespoons batter into pan, tilting pan to coat base; cook crêpe until browned lightly. Turn crêpe; brown other side. Remove crêpe from pan; cover to keep warm. Repeat with remaining batter.
4 Place rounded tablespoons of ricotta mixture in centre of each crêpe; roll to cover filling, fold in sides, continue rolling to enclose filling.

prep + cook time 40 minutes (+ standing) **makes** 8

poached pear rice pudding

1 litre (4 cups) milk
¼ cup (55g) caster sugar
⅓ cup (65g) medium-grain white rice, washed, drained
2 cups (500ml) water
1 small pear (180g), peeled, halved
1 cinnamon stick

1 Bring milk and sugar to the boil, stirring occasionally, in medium saucepan. Gradually stir in rice, reduce heat; simmer, uncovered, stirring occasionally, about 40 minutes or until rice is tender.
2 Meanwhile, bring water, pear and cinnamon to the boil in small saucepan. Reduce heat; simmer, uncovered, about 25 minutes or until pear is tender. Remove pear from liquid, chop finely; reserve 2 teaspoons pear.
3 Stir remaining pear into rice pudding. Serve pudding warm, topped with reserved pear.

prep + cook time 1 hour **serves** 6

Sprinkle with a pinch of ground cinnamon. The rice pudding can be made a day ahead, or frozen in serving sized portions for up to a month. You could also use canned fruit.

apple and raisin french toast

1 large apple (200g), peeled, cored, sliced thinly
2 tablespoons water
¼ cup (35g) coarsely chopped raisins
½ loaf unsliced white bread (320g)
3 eggs
½ cup (125ml) low-fat milk
1 tablespoon honey
½ teaspoon finely grated orange rind
½ teaspoon ground cinnamon
20g butter
2 tablespoons icing sugar

Here, french toast gets a whole new look, and it's bound to be a hit with young and old alike. Honey may contain harmful bacteria and is not recommended for children under one year old.

1 Place apple and the water in small saucepan; bring to the boil. Reduce heat; simmer, covered, about 5 minutes or until apple is just tender. Remove from heat; stir in raisins. Cool 15 minutes.

2 Meanwhile, slice bread into quarters; cut each piece three-quarters of the way through. Divide apple mixture among bread pockets.

3 Whisk eggs in medium bowl; whisk in milk, honey, rind and cinnamon.

4 Heat half the butter in large frying pan. Dip two bread pockets into egg mixture, one at a time; cook, uncovered, until browned both sides.

5 Remove from pan; cover to keep warm. Repeat with remaining butter and bread. Cut pockets into quarters; serve sprinkled with sifted icing sugar.

prep + cook time 30 minutes (+ cooling) **serves** 4

The jellies are at their best made one day ahead; they are not suitable to freeze.

You could freeze the fruit wands to make healthy ice-blocks.

Honey may contain harmful bacteria and is not recommended for children under one year old.

apple and blackcurrant jellies

1½ cups (375ml) apple and blackcurrant juice
1 tablespoon caster sugar
3 teaspoons powdered gelatine
¼ cup (60ml) water
1 small apple (130g), peeled, chopped finely

1 Stir juice and sugar in small saucepan over low heat until sugar dissolves.
2 Sprinkle gelatine over water in small heatproof jug. Stand jug in small saucepan of simmering water; stir until gelatine dissolves. Stir gelatine mixture into juice mixture.
3 Rinse inside four ½ cup (125ml) moulds with water; divide juice mixture into moulds. Divide apple into moulds. Cover; refrigerate overnight.
4 Wipe outside of moulds with hot cloth; turn jellies onto serving plates.

prep + cook time 15 minutes (+ refrigeration) **makes** 4

starry melon wands

1.5kg piece seedless watermelon, cut into 1.5cm slices
800g piece honeydew melon, cut into 1.5cm slices
1 teaspoon honey
1 cup (280g) yogurt

1 Cut out 7.5cm stars from watermelon slices; cut out 4cm stars from the centres of these stars. Cut out ten 4cm stars from honeydew melon slices.
2 Place the honeydew stars in the centre of each watermelon star. Cut off the bendy end from 10 plastic straws, push a straw through the centre of one side of the joined stars to hold the small star in position. Repeat with remaining melons and straws.
3 Combine honey and yogurt in small bowl.
4 Serve melon wands with honey yogurt for dipping.

prep time 25 minutes **makes** 10

egg-yolk custard

⅔ cup (160ml) milk
pinch ground cinnamon
1 egg yolk
2 teaspoons white sugar
1 teaspoon cornflour

1 Bring milk and cinnamon to the boil in small saucepan; remove from heat.
2 Whisk yolk, sugar and cornflour in small bowl until combined.
3 Pour milk mixture over yolk mixture, whisking continuously until combined.
4 Return mixture to same pan; cook, stirring over low heat, until mixture just boils and thickens. Remove from heat; cover surface of custard with plastic wrap. Cool to room temperature.

prep + cook time 20 minutes **makes** ¾ cup

blancmange

1 tablespoon cornflour
⅔ cup (160ml) milk
2 teaspoons sugar
¼ teaspoon vanilla essence

Store the blancmange, covered, in refrigerator, for up to 2 days

1 Blend cornflour with 1 tablespoon of the milk in a small bowl until smooth.
2 Bring remaining milk to boil in small pan; remove from heat. Add sugar, vanilla and cornflour mixture, stirring over heat until mixture boils and thickens.
3 Pour blancmange into small bowl, cover; refrigerate several hours or until set.

prep + cook time 10 minutes **makes** ⅔ cup

pikelets

1 cup (150g) self-raising flour
2 tablespoons caster sugar
1 egg, beaten lightly
¾ cup (180ml) milk, approximately

These pikelets can be stored in an airtight container, up to 2 days.

1 Combine flour and sugar in medium bowl; gradually whisk in egg and enough milk to make a thick, smooth batter.
2 Drop tablespoons of mixture into greased heated heavy-based frying pan; cook until bubbles begin to appear on surface of pikelet, turn, brown other side.
3 Serve pikelets with yogurt and a little stewed or puréed fruit or a drizzle of maple syrup.

prep + cook time 20 minutes **makes about** 22

egg-yolk custard

Mary, Mary, quite contrary

Mary, Mary, quite contrary,
How does your garden grow?
With silver bells and cockle shells,
And pretty maids all in a row.

blancmange

pikelets

Make sure you use a muesli in the apple and berry crumble that does not contain large chunks of nuts or seeds. Fresh or frozen berries can also be used. Give your toddler a few tablespoons of the warm crumble topped with custard.

apple and sultana strudel

2 tablespoons raw sugar
1 teaspoon ground cinnamon
2 sheets puff pastry, thawed
425g can pie apple
½ cup (80g) sultanas
1 egg, beaten lightly

Serve pieces of warm strudel with custard or vanilla ice-cream.

1 Preheat oven to 200°C/180°C fan-forced. Grease two oven trays.
2 Combine sugar and cinnamon in small bowl.
3 Sprinkle 2 teaspoons of the sugar mixture over one pastry sheet. Place half of the pie apple on one half of pastry sheet; sprinkle with half of the sultanas. Roll pastry carefully to enclose filling. Repeat process with another 2 teaspoons of the sugar mixture and remaining pastry sheet, pie apple and sultanas.
4 Place strudels, seam-side down, on trays; brush with egg, sprinkle each with remaining sugar mixture. Bake about 20 minutes or until browned. Stand 10 minutes before slicing.

prep + cook time 40 minutes **serves** 4

apple and berry crumble

800g can pie apple
2 cups (300g) frozen mixed berries
1 tablespoon white sugar
½ cup (125ml) water
1 cup (120g) toasted muesli
2 tablespoons plain flour
1 tablespoon brown sugar
50g butter
½ cup (20g) corn flakes

1 Preheat oven to 180°C/160°C fan-forced.
2 Place pie apple, berries, white sugar and the water in medium saucepan; bring to the boil. Reduce heat; simmer, stirring, until mixture is combined. Remove from heat.
3 Meanwhile, combine muesli, flour and brown sugar in medium bowl. Use fingertips to rub in butter; stir in cornflakes.
4 Place apple mixture in 2-litre (8 cup) ovenproof dish; sprinkle with muesli mixture. Bake, uncovered, about 20 minutes or until browned.

prep + cook time 30 minutes **serves** 6

sweet couscous

1 cup (250ml) milk
1 tablespoon couscous
1 teaspoon white sugar
pinch ground cinnamon

1 Combine ingredients in small saucepan; bring to the boil.
2 Reduce heat; simmer, stirring, about 10 minutes or until mixture thickens.

prep + cook time 20 minutes **makes** ⅓ cup

bread and butter pudding

2 slices white bread, crusts removed
butter
1¼ cups (310ml) milk
2 eggs
1 tablespoon caster sugar
¼ teaspoon vanilla essence
pinch ground nutmeg

Bread and butter pudding can be stored, covered, in the refrigerator for up to 2 days.

1 Preheat oven to 180°C/160°C fan-forced.
2 Spread bread lightly with butter; cut into small triangle-shaped pieces. Divide bread into four ½ cup (125ml) greased heatproof dishes; place dishes in baking dish.
3 Whisk milk, eggs, sugar and vanilla in medium jug; pour egg mixture over bread, sprinkle with nutmeg. Pour enough boiling water into baking dish to come halfway up sides of dishes.
4 Bake pudding, uncovered, about 20 minutes or until puddings are just set.

prep + cook time 30 minutes **serves** 4

banana fruit ice

1 medium ripe banana (200g)

This is a deliciously healthy ice-cream substitute that can be served as a snack or dessert.

1 Mash banana in small bowl; divide banana between two small freezer-safe containers. Cover; freeze several hours or overnight.
2 Just before serving, remove from freezer; stand 5 minutes. Using a fork, beat banana until light-coloured and creamy.

prep time 10 minutes (+ freezing) **makes** 2 servings

sweet couscous

bread and butter pudding

Hickory, Dickory Dock

Hickory, dickory, dock.
The mouse ran up the clock.
The clock struck one,
The mouse ran down!
Hickory, dickory, dock.

banana fruit ice

For toddlers, finely chop small pieces of muesli squares then stir through soft vanilla ice-cream or yogurt.

For the creamed rice, purée or mash a few tablespoons of the compote and stir it through a small amount of the creamed rice.

muesli squares

125g butter
⅓ cup (75g) firmly packed brown sugar
2 tablespoons honey
1 cup (90g) rolled oats
½ cup (45g) desiccated coconut
½ cup (80g) finely chopped dried apricots
½ cup (75g) finely chopped dried apples
½ cup (80g) sultanas
½ cup (75g) self-raising flour

Honey may contain harmful bacteria and is not recommended for children under one year old.

1 Preheat oven to 180°/C/160°C fan-forced. Grease and line 20cm x 30cm lamington pan.
2 Stir butter, sugar and honey in large saucepan over medium heat, without boiling, until sugar dissolves. Remove from heat; stir in remaining ingredients. Press mixture into pan.
3 Bake about 20 minutes or until golden brown. Cool in pan; cut into squares to serve.

prep + cook time 35 minutes **makes** 30

creamed rice with dried fruit compote

1 litre (4 cups) milk
⅓ cup (75g) caster sugar
10cm strip lemon rind
⅓ cup (65g) white medium-grain rice
2 teaspoons cornflour
1 tablespoon water
2 egg yolks
½ teaspoon vanilla extract

dried fruit compote
½ cup (75g) coarsely chopped dried pear
½ cup (45g) coarsely chopped dried apple
½ cup (85g) coarsely chopped seeded prunes
2 cups (500ml) water
2 tablespoons honey

Honey may contain harmful bacteria and is not recommended for children under one year old.

1 Combine milk in medium saucepan with sugar and rind; bring to the boil, stirring occasionally. Gradually stir in rice, reduce heat; simmer, covered, about 40 minutes or until rice is tender, stirring occasionally. Discard rind.
2 Meanwhile, make dried fruit compote.
3 Blend cornflour with the water in small bowl; stir in egg yolks. Stir in a heaped tablespoon of the hot creamed rice then pour egg mixture into creamed rice. Stir over medium heat until mixture boils and thickens. Stir in extract; remove from heat. Stand 15 minutes before serving with compote.

dried fruit compote Place ingredients in medium saucepan; bring to the boil. Reduce heat; simmer, uncovered, 15 minutes. Remove from heat.

prep + cook time 50 minutes (+ standing) **serves** 4

✓ 10/1/23 Good school lunch snack

abc mini muffins (apple, banana, chocolate)

¾ cup (110g) self-raising flour
⅓ cup (75g) firmly packed brown sugar
¼ cup (20g) rolled oats
1 egg
¼ cup (60ml) milk
¼ cup (60ml) apple juice
¼ cup (60ml) vegetable oil
½ medium ripe banana (100g), chopped finely
100g dark eating chocolate, grated finely

1 Preheat oven to 180°C/160°C fan-forced. Line two 12-hole mini (1 tablespoon) muffin pans with paper cases.

2 Combine flour, sugar and oats in medium bowl. Stir in combined egg, milk, juice and oil. Add banana and half of the chocolate; stir gently to just combine. Divide mixture into holes of pans.

3 Bake muffins about 15 minutes. Stand muffins in pans 5 minutes; turn onto wire rack, sprinkle with remaining chocolate.

prep + cook time 30 minutes **makes** 24

mini pineapple and carrot cakes

⅓ cup (50g) plain flour
½ cup (75g) self-raising flour
½ teaspoon bicarbonate of soda
¼ cup (55g) caster sugar
½ teaspoon ground cinnamon
225g can crushed pineapple, drained
⅔ cup (160g) firmly packed finely grated carrot
⅓ cup (80ml) vegetable oil
1 egg, beaten lightly

cream cheese icing

125g cream cheese, softened
1 tablespoon icing sugar
1 teaspoon lemon juice
2 teaspoons milk

1 Preheat oven to 180°C/160°C fan-forced. Grease two 12-hole mini (1 tablespoon) mini muffin pans.

2 Sift flours, soda, sugar and cinnamon into medium bowl. Add pineapple and carrot; stir in combined oil and egg (do not over-mix). Divide mixture into pan holes.

3 Bake muffins about 15 minutes. Stand muffins in pans 5 minutes; turn onto wire rack to cool.

4 Meanwhile, combine ingredients for cream cheese icing in small bowl. Spread cooled muffins with icing.

prep + cook time 30 minutes **makes** 24

Little Jack Horner

Little Jack Horner,
Sat in a corner,
Eating a Christmas pie,
He put in his thumb,
And pulled out a plum,
And said what a good boy am I.

the lunchbox

When lunching away from home,

whether at daycare, pre-school, kindergarten or simply an outing, kids love the excitement and anticipation of peeking into their lunchbox to discover what's inside.

Use baking paper to wrap sandwiches or wraps, and always keep them in the lunchbox with an ice brick or frozen drink container to keep them cool. Many of the recipes in this chapter can be fully or partially prepared the night before. Don't forget to freeze the drink or brick the night before as well.

Work out your children's school lunch menus for the week. Planning ahead not only saves time and money but also means you will avoid any last-minute stress. Make sandwich fillings, vegetable sticks and chopped fruit the night before and store in the fridge.

Keep clear of biscuits, muesli bars and other so-called "healthy" treats. Most of them are loaded with sugar and/or fat.

vegetable rice paper rolls

1 large carrot (180g), grated coarsely
2 stalks celery (300g), trimmed, chopped finely
150g wombok, shredded finely
2 teaspoons fish sauce
2 teaspoons brown sugar
1 tablespoon lemon juice
24 x 17cm-square rice paper sheets
24 fresh mint leaves

1 Combine carrot, celery, wombok, sauce, sugar and juice in small bowl.
2 Place 1 sheet of rice paper in medium bowl of warm water until just softened; lift sheet carefully from water, placing it on a tea-towel-covered board with a corner pointing towards you. Place 1 level tablespoon of the vegetable mixture horizontally in centre of sheet; top with 1 mint leaf. Fold corner facing you over filling; roll rice paper to enclose filling, folding in sides after first complete turn of roll. Repeat with remaining rice paper sheets, vegetable mixture and mint leaves.

prep + cook time 45 minutes **makes** 24

tofu and buk choy rice paper rolls

12 fresh baby corn, halved horizontally
24 baby buk choy leaves
300g firm silken tofu
2 cups (160g) bean sprouts
24 x 17cm-square rice paper sheets

chilli sauce

⅓ cup (80ml) sweet chilli sauce
1 tablespoon soy sauce

1 Boil, steam or microwave corn and buk choy, separately, until tender; drain.
2 Meanwhile, combine ingredients for chilli sauce in small bowl.
3 Halve tofu horizontally; cut each half into 12 even strips. Place tofu in medium bowl with half of the chilli sauce.
4 Place 1 sheet of rice paper in medium bowl of warm water until just softened; lift sheet carefully from water, placing it on a tea-towel-covered board with a corner pointing towards you. Place one tofu strip horizontally in centre of sheet; top with one piece of corn then a buk choy leaf and a few sprouts. Fold corner facing you over filling; roll rice paper to enclose filling, folding in one side after first complete turn of roll. Repeat with remaining rice paper sheets, tofu, corn, buk choy and sprouts. Serve rolls with remaining chilli sauce.

prep + cook time 45 minutes **makes** 24

Baa Baa Black Sheep

Baa, baa, black sheep
Have you any wool?
Yes sir, yes sir.
Three bags full;
One for the master,
And one for the dame,
And one for the little boy
Who lives down the lane.

hummus and cucumber sandwich

tuna and sweet corn sandwich

fruit and nut sandwich

peanut butter and vegies sandwich

hummus and cucumber sandwich

Spread one slice of bread with 1 tablespoon prepared hummus; top with a quarter of a thinly sliced lebanese cucumber and another slice of bread.

prep time 10 minutes **makes** 1

tuna and sweet corn sandwich

Combine half of a drained 185g can tuna in springwater, 2 tablespoons drained and rinsed canned sweet corn kernels, and 1 tablespoon mayonnaise in small bowl. Spread mixture on one slice of bread. Top with a quarter of a thinly sliced lebanese cucumber and another slice of bread.

prep time 10 minutes **makes** 1

fruit and nut sandwich

Spread one slice of bread with 3 teaspoons hazelnut chocolate spread; top with 1 tablespoon sultanas and half of a thinly sliced small banana. Top with another slice of bread.

prep time 10 minutes **makes** 1

peanut butter and vegies sandwich

Spread 1 tablespoon peanut butter over two slices of bread; top one slice with 1 tablespoon coarsely grated carrot and 1 tablespoon coarsely grated celery. Top with remaining bread slice.

prep time 10 minutes **makes** 1

Peanuts can cause reactions in some children – they are not recommended for children under one year old.

hummus

2 x 300g cans chickpeas, rinsed and drained
2 tablespoons olive oil
2 teaspoons lemon juice
1 clove garlic, crushed
1 cup (280g) yogurt

1 Cook chickpeas in medium saucepan of boiling water, uncovered, about 15 minutes or until tender; drain. Cool 10 minutes.
2 Blend or process chickpeas with oil, juice, garlic and yogurt until smooth.
3 Serve hummus with pitta bread triangles.

prep + cook time 25 minutes **makes** 2 cups

carrot dip

5 medium carrots (600g), chopped coarsely
1 tablespoon olive oil
1 clove garlic, crushed
½ teaspoon ground cumin
2 teaspoons lemon juice
⅓ cup (95g) yogurt

1 Boil, steam or microwave carrot until tender; drain.
2 Heat oil in large frying pan; cook garlic and cumin, stirring, until fragrant. Stir in carrot and juice; cook, stirring, until combined. Remove from heat; cool 10 minutes.
3 Blend or process carrot mixture and yogurt until just smooth.
4 Serve carrot dip with grissini sticks.

prep + cook time 35 minutes **makes** 1½ cups

Pat a cake

Pat a cake, pat a cake,
baker's man,
Bake me a cake
as fast as you can.
Pat it and prick it
and mark it with B,
And put it in the oven
for baby and me.

cheese and salad sandwich

Combine 200g low-fat cottage cheese, ⅓ cup coarsely grated reduced-fat cheddar cheese, 1 cup shredded baby spinach leaves, 1 thinly sliced green onion, 1 finely grated small carrot, 1 tablespoon roasted sesame seeds and 2 teaspoons lemon juice in medium bowl. Divide 30g mesclun and between four slices of wholemeal bread and spread with cheese mixture; top with another four slices of wholemeal bread. Cut sandwiches into squares.

prep time 10 minutes
makes 12 squares

corn, zucchini and egg sandwich

Combine 2 tablespoons canned corn kernels, ½ small coarsely grated zucchini, 2 teaspoons mayonnaise and 1 mashed hard-boiled egg in small bowl. Spread egg mixture on one slice of sandwich bread; top with another slice of sandwich bread. Cut into squares or triangles.

prep time 10 minutes
makes 4 squares

chicken, celery and avocado sandwich

Combine ⅓ cup finely shredded cooked chicken, 1 trimmed finely chopped celery stalk, ¼ small avocado and 1 teaspoon lemon juice in small bowl. Spread chicken mixture on one slice of sandwich bread; top with another slice of sandwich bread. Cut into squares or triangles.

prep time 10 minutes
makes 4 squares

ricotta and honey sandwiches

Combine ½ cup ricotta cheese, 1 tablespoon honey and ¼ cup finely chopped dried pears in small bowl. Spread ricotta mixture on 3 slices of raisin bread; top with another 3 slices of raisin bread. Discard crusts; cut sandwiches into squares.

prep time 10 minutes
makes 12 squares

blt

Cook 2 finely chopped rindless bacon rashers in small heated frying pan, stirring, until browned and crisp; drain on absorbent paper. Combine bacon with 2 finely chopped hard-boiled eggs and 2 tablespoons of mayonnaise in small bowl. Spread another 2 tablespoons of mayonnaise on four slices of bread, then top with ½ cup coarsely shredded butter lettuce and 1 small thinly sliced tomato; top with egg mixture and another four slices of bread. Discard crusts; cut sandwiches into fingers.

prep + cook time 25 minutes
makes 12 fingers

chicken, avocado and cream cheese sandwich

Combine ¼ cup (40g) coarsely chopped barbecued chicken meat, a quarter of a coarsely chopped small avocado, and 1 teaspoon lemon juice in small bowl. Spread 1 tablespoon spreadable cream cheese on one slice of bread; top with chicken mixture, ¼ cup loosely packed mixed salad leaves, and another slice of bread.

prep time 10 minutes **makes** 1

cheese and vegies sandwich

Combine 2 tablespoons coarsely grated cheddar cheese, 2 tablespoons coarsely grated carrot, 2 tablespoons coarsely grated celery, and 1 tablespoon sour cream in small bowl. Spread mixture over one slice of bread; top with another slice of bread.

prep time 10 minutes **makes** 1

egg, tomato and mayonnaise sandwich

Combine half of a seeded, finely chopped small tomato, 1 tablespoon coarsely grated cheddar cheese, one coarsely chopped hard-boiled egg, and 1 tablespoon mayonnaise in small bowl. Spread mixture on one slice of bread; top with ¼ cup loosely packed mixed lettuce leaves and another slice of bread.

prep time 10 minutes **makes** 1

cheese, sausage and pickle sandwich

Spread 1 tablespoon of sweet mustard pickle over two slices of bread; top one slice of bread with one slice of cheddar cheese and one cold cooked thickly sliced beef sausage. Top with remaining slice of bread.

prep time 10 minutes **makes** 1

chicken, avocado and cream cheese sandwich

cheese and vegies sandwich

egg, tomato and mayonnaise sandwich

cheese, sausage and pickle sandwich

Wee Willie Winkie

Wee Willie Winkie runs
through the town,
Upstairs and downstairs,
in his nightgown.
Rapping at the window,
crying throught the lock,
"Are the children all in bed,
for now it's eight o'clock."

prawn and avocado rice paper rolls

24 cooked medium king prawns (1.1kg)
2 tablespoons mayonnaise
24 x 17cm-square rice paper sheets
1 large avocado (320g), sliced thinly
80g snow pea sprouts, trimmed

1 Shell and devein prawns; chop coarsely. Combine prawns and mayonnaise in small bowl.
2 Place 1 sheet of rice paper in medium bowl of warm water until just softened; lift sheet carefully from water, placing it on a tea-towel-covered board with a corner pointing towards you. Place 1 level tablespoon of the prawn mixture horizontally in centre of rice paper; top with a little of the avocado then a few sprouts. Fold corner facing you over filling; roll rice paper to enclose filling, folding in one side after first complete turn of roll. Repeat with remaining rice paper sheets, prawn mixture, avocado and sprouts.

prep time 30 minutes **makes** 24

teriyaki chicken rice paper rolls

6 chicken thigh fillets (660g), trimmed
¼ cup (60ml) thick teriyaki marinade
2 tablespoons water
2 lebanese cucumbers (260g)
2 teaspoons vegetable oil
24 x 17cm-square rice paper sheets
200g enoki mushrooms, trimmed

1 Slice each chicken thigh into eight strips lengthways. Combine chicken, teriyaki and the water in small bowl, cover; refrigerate 1 hour. Drain chicken; discard marinade.
2 Meanwhile, cut cucumbers in half lengthways; discard seeds. Cut cucumber halves in half crossways; cut pieces into three strips lengthways.
3 Heat oil in large frying pan; cook chicken, in batches, until cooked through. Cool 10 minutes.
4 Place 1 sheet of rice paper in medium bowl of warm water until just softened; lift sheet carefully from water, placing it on a tea-towel-covered board with a corner pointing towards you. Place two pieces of chicken horizontally in centre of rice paper; top with one piece of cucumber then a few mushrooms. Fold corner facing you over filling; roll rice paper to enclose filling, folding in one side after first complete turn of roll. Repeat with remaining rice paper sheets, chicken, cucumber and mushrooms.

prep + cook time 45 minutes (+ refrigeration) **makes** 24

✓22/1/21 – For my Australia Day Party with the Kuhlmans

vegemite and cheese pinwheels

Preheat oven to 200°C/180°C fan-forced. Oil 19cm x 30cm lamington pan. Sift 2 cups self-raising flour and 1 tablespoon caster sugar into medium bowl; rub in 50g chopped butter. Stir in ¾ cup milk, mix to a soft sticky dough. Turn dough onto floured surface; knead lightly until smooth. Roll dough to 30cm x 40cm shape. Spread 2 tablespoons vegemite over dough; sprinkle with 1¼ cups coarsely grated cheddar cheese. Starting from long side, roll dough firmly; trim ends. Cut roll into 12 slices; place pinwheels, cut-side up, in single layer, in pan. Bake about 30 minutes. Serve pinwheels warm.

prep + cook time 40 minutes
makes 12

spinach and cheese monster scones

Preheat oven to 240°C/220°C fan-forced. Oil deep 20cm-square cake pan. Thaw a 250g packet of finely chopped frozen spinach; squeeze out excess liquid. Sift 2½ cups self-raising flour and 1 tablespoon caster sugar into medium bowl; rub in 50g chopped butter. Stir in ½ cup coarsely grated cheddar cheese and the spinach. Stir in ¾ cup milk, mix to a soft sticky dough. Turn dough onto floured surface; knead lightly until smooth. Press dough out to 2cm thickness. Cut 16 x 4.5cm rounds from dough. Place scones, just touching, in pan. Bake about 20 minutes. Serve warm.

prep + cook time 30 minutes
makes 16

apple and cinnamon mini muffins

Preheat oven to 180°C/160°C fan-forced. Line two 12-hole (1-tablespoon/20ml) mini muffin pans with paper cases. Sift ¾ cup self-raising flour and 1 teaspoon ground cinnamon into medium bowl; stir in ⅓ cup firmly packed brown sugar and ¼ cup rolled oats. Stir in combined ¼ cup milk, ¼ cup apple juice, ¼ cup vegetable oil and 1 egg. Add ¼ cup coarsely grated, peeled apple; stir gently to combine. Divide mixture into paper cases. Bake muffins about 15 minutes. Stand 5 minutes before turning, top-side up, onto wire rack to cool.

prep + cook time 25 minutes
makes 24

fruit and cereal snack mix

Preheat oven to 180°C/160°C fan-forced. Combine ½ cup rice bubbles, ½ cup cornflakes and 1 cup flaked coconut in large shallow baking dish; roast, uncovered, about 5 minutes, stirring occasionally. Transfer to large bowl; cool. Stir in ½ cup finely chopped dried pear, ⅓ cup finely chopped dried apple, ¼ cup finely chopped seeded prunes and ½ cup dried cranberries.

prep + cook time 20 minutes (+ cooling) **makes** 3½ cups
Store in an airtight container in refrigerator for up to 1 month. Change the fruit to suit your child's taste. We've allowed ¼ cup of the snack per serving.

chicken and corn dip

Bring 2 cups water to the boil in small saucepan; add one 200g chicken breast fillet. Reduce heat; simmer, covered, about 10 minutes or until chicken is cooked. Cool chicken in liquid 10 minutes; drain. Shred chicken finely using two forks. Combine chicken, 250g cream cheese, 2 x 125g cans creamed corn, 2 tablespoons finely chopped fresh flat-leaf parsley and 1 tablespoon finely chopped fresh chives in medium bowl.

prep + cook time 20 minutes (+ cooling) **makes** 2½ cups
Serve dip with toasted torn pitta bread, vegetable sticks or crackers. Use any leftover dip as a sandwich filling. This recipe is not suitable for freezing.

muesli slice

Preheat oven to 160°C/140°C fan-forced. Grease 24cm x 32cm swiss roll pan; line base with baking paper, extending paper 5cm over long sides. Combine 1½ cups cornflakes, 1½ cups rolled oats, 1 cup rice bubbles, ½ cup shredded coconut and 400g can skim sweetened condensed milk in large bowl; press mixture firmly into pan. Bake about 40 minutes or until browned lightly; cool in pan. Lift slice from pan; cut slice into bars.

prep + cook time 50 minutes (+ cooling) **makes** 24

The slice will keep in an airtight container for up to a week or, can be frozen for a month.

rhubarb, muesli and yogurt cups

Bring 2 cups coarsely chopped fresh or frozen rhubarb, ¼ cup caster sugar, ½ cup water and ½ teaspoon ground cinnamon to the boil in medium saucepan. Reduce heat; simmer, uncovered, stirring occasionally, about 10 minutes or until rhubarb is tender. Transfer to medium heatproof bowl, cover; refrigerate 1 hour. Divide rhubarb mixture among four ¾-cup (180ml) serving glasses; top with 1⅓ cups low-fat vanilla yogurt then ⅓ cup toasted muesli.

prep + cook time 20 minutes (+ refrigeration) **serves** 4

You will need about four trimmed rhubarb stalks for this recipe.

ham, egg and cheese toastie

Spread 2 slices wholemeal bread with 1 tablespoon barbecue sauce. Top one bread slice with 30g shaved ham, 1 sliced hard-boiled egg and ¼ cup coarsely grated reduced-fat cheddar cheese then remaining bread slice. Toast in sandwich press until golden brown.

prep + cook time 10 minutes
serves 1

fruit skewers with honey yogurt

Thread ½ medium peeled and cored, pineapple cut into 2.5cm lengths then crossways into 3cm pieces alternately with 2 large peeled and segmented oranges, 250g hulled strawberries halved crossways and 2 large peeled bananas cut into 3cm slices onto twelve 20cm wooden skewers; place on oven tray. Stir 30g butter, ¼ cup brown sugar and 1 tablespoon lemon juice in small saucepan over low heat until butter melts and sugar dissolves. Pour mixture over skewers, coating all fruit pieces. Cook, in batches, on heated greased grill plate (or grill or barbecue) about 5 minutes or until browned. Serve skewers with 1 cup honey yogurt.

prep + cook time 40 minutes
serves 4

ham and cheese pinwheels

Preheat oven to 200°C/180°C fan-forced. Oil 19cm x 29cm slice pan. Cook 6 lightly beaten eggs in oiled medium frying pan over low heat, stirring constantly, until scrambled. Sift 2 cups self-raising flour and 1 tablespoon caster sugar into medium bowl; rub in 30g butter. Stir in ¾ cup low-fat milk; mix to a soft, sticky dough. Knead dough on floured surface; roll into 30cm x 40cm shape. Spread ¼ cup tomato paste over dough; sprinkle with 175g thin strips of shaved ham, egg and 1 cup coarsely grated reduced-fat cheddar cheese. Starting from long side, roll dough firmly; trim ends. Cut roll into 12 slices; place, cut-side up, in single layer, in pan. Bake about 30 minutes. Serve pinwheels warm.

prep + cook time 1 hour **makes** 12

peanut butter and alfalfa sandwich

Peanuts can cause reactions in some children – they are not recommended for children under one year old. If your child's school has a nut-free policy, peanut butter will need to be avoided.

Spread two slices of wholemeal bread with 1 tablespoon smooth peanut butter; top one slice with ¼ cup alfalfa sprouts and 1 teaspoon sunflower seed kernels. Top with remaining bread, peanut butter-side down. Remove and discard crusts; cut sandwich into triangles.

prep time 5 minutes **makes** 1

beef, cheese and carrot sandwich

Combine ½ small coarsely grated carrot, 2 tablespoons spreadable cream cheese and 2 tablespoons finely shredded iceberg lettuce in small bowl. Spread half of the carrot mixture on one slice of sandwich bread; top with ¼ cup finely chopped roast beef, remaining carrot mixture and another slice of sandwich bread. Cut into triangles or squares.

prep time 10 minutes **makes** 1

carrot, sultana and cottage cheese sandwich

Combine ½ small coarsely grated carrot, 1 tablespoon cottage cheese and 2 teaspoons sultanas in small bowl. Spread one slice of white bread with cheese mixture; top with a second slice of white bread. Remove and discard crusts; cut sandwich into fingers.

prep time 5 minutes **makes** 1

tuna and baby spinach sandwich

For children under one year old, peel and remove seeds from tomato before chopping. We used tuna slices from a 95g can tuna slices in springwater.

Combine ¼ cup coarsely chopped baby spinach leaves, 1 tablespoon mayonnaise and ¼ small finely chopped tomato in small bowl. Spread one slice of white bread with half the spinach mixture; top with 3 drained tuna slices in springwater, remaining spinach mixture and a second slice of white bread. Cut sandwich using large fish cutter.

prep time 5 minutes **makes** 1

peanut butter and alfalfa sandwich

beef, cheese and carrot sandwich

carrot, sultana and cottage cheese sandwich

tuna and baby spinach sandwich

Lavash is a soft, yeast-free flat bread available, white or wholegrain, from most supermarkets. It is the ideal bread choice for these lunchbox roll ups.

The frittata can be eaten cold or warm. Store frittata slices, in an airtight container, in the refrigerator for up to three days.

turkey and cream cheese roll ups

1 piece lavash bread
1 tablespoon spreadable cream cheese
3 slices (65g) turkey
3 cheese slices
3 iceberg lettuce leaves
1 small (60g) egg tomato, sliced thinly

1 Just before serving, spread bread with cream cheese. Place turkey, cheese, lettuce and tomato on bread; roll tightly then cut in half.

prep time 10 minutes **makes** 2

baked potato, ham and cheese frittata

4 medium potatoes (800g)
4 eggs, beaten lightly
½ cup (90g) finely chopped leg ham
1 medium tomato (150g), chopped finely
2 green onions, sliced thinly
1 tablespoon finely chopped fresh flat-leaf parsley
1 cup (120g) coarsely grated cheddar

1 At home, a day ahead, preheat oven to 180°C/160°C fan-forced. Oil shallow 1.5-litre (6 cup) ovenproof dish.
2 Grate potatoes coarsely; squeeze out excess water.
3 Combine potato, egg, ham, tomato, onion, parsley and half of the cheese in medium bowl. Spread mixture into dish; sprinkle with remaining cheese.
4 Bake frittata about 40 minutes or until browned. Cool to room temperature, then cut into squares; refrigerate until cold.

prep + cook time 1 hour **serves** 4

food for allergies

A child with food allergies can

feel seriously left out, especially at parties, and unfortunately, the prevalence of allergies in children is rising. The foods that are most commonly associated with causing allergic reactions are milk, egg, peanuts, tree nuts, gluten and shellfish. Thankfully, there are many substitutes and alternatives available that you may use in place of these offenders. It's possible, and important, to make delicious food that not only your child will like but that all your child's friends will like as well. That way they won't feel 'different' from their friends. The recipes here are for good-looking and good-tasting food that doesn't look in the least like 'special' food.

semi-dried tomato and spinach tart

300ml light thickened cream
2 tablespoons milk
4 eggs
½ cup (80g) coarsely shredded cooked chicken
¼ cup (35g) drained semi-dried tomatoes, chopped finely
25g baby spinach leaves, torn coarsely

gluten-free pastry
1 cup (180g) rice flour
¼ cup (35g) (corn) cornflour
¼ cup (30g) soya flour
170g cold butter, chopped coarsely
2 tablespoons cold water, approximately

This recipe is gluten-free, wheat-free and nut-free.

We found it necessary to grease the tin well with butter. The tart is best made and eaten warm or cold on the same day; it is not suitable to freeze. The pastry can be made 2 days ahead, and refrigerated, or frozen for up to a month.

1 Make gluten-free pastry.
2 Preheat oven to 220°C/200°C fan-forced. Grease 11cm x 34cm loose-based fluted flan tin with melted butter.
3 Roll pastry between sheets of baking paper until 5mm thick. Ease pastry into tin, press into base and sides; trim edge, prick base with fork.
4 Bake pastry case about 15 minutes or until browned lightly. Cool pastry case. Reduce oven temperature to 200°C/180°C fan-forced.
5 Meanwhile, whisk cream, milk and eggs in medium jug. Fill pastry case with chicken, tomato and spinach; pour in the egg mixture. Bake tart about 25 minutes.

gluten-free pastry Process flours and butter until mixture is crumbly. Add enough of the water to make ingredients come together. Knead dough gently and lightly on floured surface until smooth.

prep + cook time 1 hour 10 minutes **serves** 10

Serve pudding with cream or ice-cream. Puddings can be made in either texas muffin pans or individual ovenproof dishes – they will take about 20 minutes to cook. This recipe can be made up to 4 hours ahead of serving and is best served warm; pudding is not suitable to freeze.

saucy caramel pudding

1 cup (135g) gluten-free self-raising flour
⅓ cup (75g) firmly packed brown sugar
20g butter, melted
½ cup (125ml) milk

caramel sauce
1⅓ cups (330ml) water
⅓ cup (75g) firmly packed brown sugar
30g butter

This recipe is gluten-free, wheat-free and egg-free.

1 Preheat oven to 180°C/160°C fan-forced. Grease deep 1-litre (4-cup) ovenproof dish.
2 Combine sifted four, sugar, butter and milk in medium bowl. Pour mixture into dish.
3 Make caramel sauce.
4 Pour sauce slowly over back of spoon evenly onto mixture in dish. Bake pudding about 50 minutes. Stand at least 10 minutes before serving.

caramel sauce Stir ingredients in small saucepan, over medium heat, without boiling, until smooth.

prep + cook time 1 hour (+ standing) **serves** 4

berry crumbles with frozen yogurt

1 cup (150g) fresh or frozen mixed berries
2 tablespoons strawberry-flavoured frozen yogurt

crumble topping
2 tablespoons puffed rice
1 tablespoon gluten-free plain flour
1 tablespoon brown rice flour
1 tablespoon brown sugar
15g butter

This recipe is gluten-free, wheat-free, yeast-free and egg-free.

For a dairy-free version as well, substitute fruit-flavoured soy yogurt for the frozen yogurt and dairy-free spread for the butter. The crumbles are best made and served on the same day; they're not suitable to freeze.

1 Preheat oven to 200°C/180°C fan-forced. Grease two ¾ cup (180ml) ovenproof dishes.
2 Make crumble topping.
3 Divide berries into dishes; sprinkle with crumble topping. Bake about 30 minutes or until browned lightly.
4 Serve crumbles warm with frozen yogurt.

crumble topping Blend or process puffed rice until fine, add flours, sugar and butter; blend until crumbly.

prep + cook time 50 minutes **makes** 2

savoury buckwheat pancakes

1 cup (150g) buckwheat flour
½ cup (60g) gluten-free plain flour
3 teaspoons gluten-free baking powder
2 eggs
2 cups (500ml) buttermilk
50g butter, melted
1 medium zucchini (120g), grated coarsely
1 small carrot (70g), grated coarsely
½ cup (80g) fresh or frozen corn kernels

This recipe is gluten-free, wheat-free and nut-free.

1 Sift flours and baking powder into large bowl; gradually whisk in combined eggs and buttermilk until smooth. Stir in butter and vegetables.

2 Heat lightly oiled small frying pan; pour ⅓ cup of the batter into pan. Cook pancake until bubbles appear on surface. Turn pancake; cook, until browned lightly. Repeat with remaining batter.

prep + cook time 30 minutes **makes** 10

macaroni cheese with peas

250g packet gluten-free spiral pasta
2 tablespoons dairy-free spread
2 tablespoons (corn) cornflour
1½ cups (375ml) water
1 cup (250ml) soy milk
½ cup (60g) coarsely grated soy cheese
1 cup (120g) frozen baby peas
½ cup (35g) stale gluten-free breadcrumbs

This recipe is gluten-free, wheat-free, dairy-free and nut-free.

This recipe is best made and eaten as soon as it's cool enough; it's not suitable to freeze.

1 Preheat oven to 200°C/180°C fan-forced.

2 Cook pasta in large saucepan of boiling water until tender; drain.

3 Meanwhile, melt spread in large saucepan; stir in cornflour, cook, stirring 1 minute. Gradually add the combined water and milk, stirring constantly, until mixture boils and thickens slightly. Remove from heat; stir in cheese, peas and pasta.

4 Pour mixture into oiled shallow 1.5 litre (6 cup) ovenproof dish; sprinkle with breadcrumbs. Bake about 25 minutes. Cool before serving.

prep + cook time 50 minutes **serves** 6

Hey Diddle Diddle

Hey diddle diddle,
The cat and the fiddle,
The cow jumped over the moon,
The little dog laughed
to see such fun,
And the dish ran away
with the spoon.

melonade

Stir ½ cup lemon juice and 2 tablespoons caster sugar in small saucepan over low heat until sugar dissolves. Cool. Blend or process 3 cups coarsely chopped watermelon, in batches, until smooth; strain through sieve into large jug. Stir in lemon syrup and 1½ cups chilled sparkling mineral water; serve immediately.

prep time 10 minutes (+ standing)
makes 1 litre (4 cups)
You need a 1kg piece of watermelon for this recipe.

papaya, strawberry and orange juice

Blend 1 large coarsely chopped papaya with 250g strawberries and ¾ cup fresh orange juice until smooth; serve immediately.

prep time 10 minutes
makes 1 litre (4 cups)
Refrigerate all ingredients before making the juice. Serve the juice within 30 minutes of making.

passionfruit sparkler

Freeze 2 x 170g cans passionfruit in syrup in ice-cube trays. Combine passionfruit cubes with 1 medium segemented orange, 150g halved seedless red grapes, 1½ cups pineapple juice, 1½ cups orange juice and 1 cup sparkling mineral water in large jug.

prep time 10 minutes (+ freezing)
makes 1 litre (4 cups)

peach and raspberry juice

Blend or process 1 large peeled and coarsely chopped peach with ¼ cup fresh or frozen raspberries until smooth; pour into glass. Stir in ½ cup water; serve with ice.

prep time 5 minutes
makes 1 cup (250ml)

pineapple juice with watermelon ice

Blend or process 280g coarsely chopped seedless watermelon until smooth. Using back of large spoon, push through sieve; discard solids. Pour juice into ice-cube tray; freeze until set. Push 650g coarsely chopped pineapple and 4 peeled large oranges through juice extractor. Divide juice among serving glasses; top with watermelon ice-cubes.

prep time 10 minutes (+ freezing)
makes 1.25 litres (5 cups)

You need a 550g piece of watermelon and half a large pineapple weighing about 1kg for this recipe.

potato and oregano pizza

375g packet gluten-free bread mix
300g baby new potatoes, sliced thinly
2 teaspoons finely chopped fresh oregano
2 teaspoons olive oil
1 clove garlic, crushed

This recipe is gluten-free, wheat-free, yeast-free, dairy-free and nut-free.

1 Preheat oven to 220°C/200°C fan-forced. Oil two 25cm x 35cm swiss roll pans; line bases with baking paper, extending paper 5cm over long sides.
2 Make bread mix according to packet directions; spread mixture into pans.
3 Combine remaining ingredients in medium bowl; spread potato mixture over bread mix.
4 Bake pizzas about 20 minutes or until potato is tender and bases are crisp.

prep + cook time 45 minutes **serves** 6

cheesy corn and chicken loaves

⅓ cup (6g) puffed millet
900g chicken mince
1 clove garlic, crushed
1 egg
¾ cup (120g) fresh or frozen corn kernels
½ cup (60g) coarsely grated cheddar cheese
¼ cup coarsely chopped fresh chives

This recipe is gluten-free, wheat-free and nut-free.

You will need 1 corn cob (400g). Serve loaves with steamed mixed vegetables. Loaves can be served warm or cold. They can be made a day ahead, but are not suitable to freeze.

1 Preheat oven to 220°C/200°C fan-forced. Oil 8-hole ½ cup (125ml) petite loaf pan.
2 Blend or process millet until fine. Combine mince, garlic, egg, corn, cheese, millet and 2 tablespoons of the chives in large bowl. Divide mixture into pan holes.
3 Bake loaves 10 minutes; remove from oven. Sprinkle with remaining chives; bake further 10 minutes or until cooked through.

prep + cook time 35 minutes **makes** 8

Pizza slices can be stored in an airtight container in the refrigerator for up to 2 days. Pizza slices can be eaten cold or reheated in the microwave on high (100%) for about 30 seconds.

Quesadillas are best made and eaten as soon as they're cool enough to handle. They are not suitable to freeze.

Serve the fish and chips with lemon wedges. This recipe is best made, cooked and eaten as soon as it's cool enough.

quesadillas

This recipe is dairy-free, egg-free and nut-free.

2 medium tomatoes (300g), seeded, chopped finely
1 medium avocado (250g), chopped finely
1 medium zucchini (120g), grated coarsely
½ small red onion (50g), chopped finely
125g can corn kernels, rinsed, drained
425g can mexe-style beans, rinsed, drained
1 cup (130g) coarsely grated soy cheese
8 small corn tortillas (250g)

1 Preheat sandwich press.
2 Combine vegetables and beans in medium bowl.
3 Divide bean mixture and the cheese over four tortillas, leaving 2cm border around edge; top each with the remaining tortillas.
4 Cook quesadillas, one at a time, in sandwich press until browned lightly. Cut into quarters.

prep + cook time 30 minutes **makes** 4

rice-crumbed fish and chips

This recipe is gluten-free, wheat-free, dairy-free and egg-free.

Rice flakes are available from health food shops and supermarkets.

1 medium potato (200g)
⅓ cup (20g) rice flakes
2 teaspoons finely chopped fresh flat-leaf parsley
1 teaspoon finely grated lemon rind
180g firm white fish fillet, halved lengthways
cooking-oil spray

1 Preheat oven to 220°C/200°C fan-forced.
2 Cut potato into 1cm slices; cut slices into 1cm chips. Place chips on baking-paper-lined oven tray; bake about 35 minutes or until browned lightly.
3 Meanwhile, coarsely crush rice flakes in small bowl; mix in parsley and rind. Press crumb mixture onto both sides of fish; spray fish with cooking-oil spray for about 2 seconds each side.
4 Place fish on tray; cook fish in oven for final 10 minutes of chip-cooking time.
5 Divide fish and chips between two serving plates.

prep + cook time 1 hour **serves** 2

chocolate-on-chocolate cakes

200g butter, softened
2¼ cups (300g) gluten-free self-raising flour
¼ cup (25g) cocoa powder
1 cup (220g) caster sugar
¾ cup (180ml) milk
2 eggs
2 egg whites

chocolate icing
1 cup (160g) pure icing sugar
1 tablespoon cocoa powder
2 tablespoons water

This recipe is gluten-free, wheat-free and yeast-free.

Store cakes in an airtight container for up to two days. Uniced cakes can be frozen for up to two months.
For a dairy-free version of this cake, substitute dairy-free spread for the butter and soy milk for the milk; the rest of the recipe stays the same.

1 Preheat oven to 180°C/160°C fan-forced. Line two 12-hole (⅓ cup/80ml) muffin pans with paper cases.
2 Beat butter in large bowl with electric mixer until pale. Beat sifted flour, cocoa and ¼ cup of the caster sugar alternately with milk into butter, in two batches, until combined.
3 Beat eggs and egg whites in small bowl with electric mixer until thick and creamy. Gradually add remaining caster sugar, one tablespoon at a time, beating until sugar dissolves between additions. Gradually beat egg mixture into flour mixture until combined.
4 Drop 2½ tablespoons mixture into each paper case; bake cakes about 20 minutes. Turn, top-side-up, onto wire rack to cool.
5 Meanwhile, make chocolate icing.
6 Spread cold cakes with chocolate icing.
chocolate icing Sift sugar and cocoa into small bowl; stir in water.

prep + cook time 40 minutes (+ cooling) **makes** 24

For the porridge, you can substitute the rice milk for soy, whole or skim milk.

The muffins can be stored in airtight container in refrigerator for up to 2 days or freezer for up to 1 month.

rolled rice porridge

1½ cups (160g) rolled rice
1.125 litres (4½ cups) water
⅓ cup (80ml) rice milk
⅓ cup (50g) coarsely chopped dried apricots
¼ cup (10g) flaked coconut, toasted
2 tablespoons honey

This recipe is gluten-free, wheat-free, yeast-free, dairy-free, egg-free and nut-free.

1 Combine rolled rice and 3 cups of the water in medium bowl. Cover; stand at room temperature overnight.
2 Place undrained rolled rice in medium saucepan; cook, stirring, until mixture comes to the boil. Add the remaining water; bring to the boil. Reduce heat; simmer, uncovered, for about 5 minutes or until thickened.
3 Divide porridge and milk among serving bowls. Sprinkle with apricots and coconut; drizzle with honey.

prep + cook time 20 minutes (+ standing) **serves** 4

mini corn and chive muffins

1¼ cups (175g) gluten-free self-raising flour
90g butter, melted
2 eggs, beaten lightly
2 x 125g cans gluten-free creamed corn
½ cup (50g) pizza cheese
2 tablespoons finely chopped fresh chives

This recipe is gluten-free, wheat-free, yeast-free and nut-free.

1 Preheat oven to 200°C/180°C fan-forced. Oil two 12-hole (1-tablespoon/20ml) mini muffin pans.
2 Sift flour into medium bowl; stir in butter, eggs, corn, cheese and chives. Divide mixture into pan holes.
3 Bake muffins about 15 minutes. Stand muffins in pan 5 minutes; turn onto wire rack to cool.

prep + cook time 30 minutes **makes** 24

coconut custard tarts

1½ cups (120g) desiccated coconut
1½ cups (115g) shredded coconut
⅔ cup (150g) caster sugar
4 egg whites, beaten lightly
3 egg yolks
½ cup (110g) caster sugar, extra
1 tablespoon arrowroot
¾ cup (180ml) milk
½ cup (125ml) cream
1 vanilla bean
5cm strip lemon rind
1 tablespoon pure icing sugar

This recipe is gluten-free, wheat-free and yeast-free.

Tarts can be stored in an airtight container in the refrigerator for up to 2 days.

1 Preheat oven to 180°C/160°C fan-forced. Grease 12-hole (⅓-cup/80ml) muffin pan.
2 Combine coconuts and sugar in large bowl; stir in egg whites. Press mixture over base and side of pan holes to make cases.
3 Whisk egg yolks, extra sugar and arrowroot together in medium saucepan; gradually whisk in milk and cream to make custard.
4 Split vanilla bean in half lengthways; scrape seeds into custard, discard pod. Add lemon rind to custard; stir over medium heat until mixture boils and thickens slightly. Remove from heat immediately; discard rind.
5 Spoon warm custard into pastry cases; bake about 15 minutes or until set and browned lightly. Stand tarts in pan for 10 minutes. Transfer to wire rack to cool.
6 Serve tarts dusted with sifted icing sugar.

prep + cook time 45 minutes (+ standing & cooling) **makes** 12

coconut rice puddings

4 eggs
⅓ cup (75g) caster sugar
1 teaspoon vanilla extract
400ml can coconut cream
1½ cups (375ml) gluten-free soy milk
1 cup cooked white medium-grain rice
½ cup (80g) sultanas
½ teaspoon ground cinnamon

This recipe is gluten-free, wheat-free, yeast-free and dairy-free.

1 Preheat oven to 180°C/160°C fan-forced. Grease six ¾-cup (180ml) ovenproof dishes.
2 Whisk eggs, sugar and extract in large jug until combined; whisk in cream and soy milk. Stir in rice and sultanas. Divide mixture evenly among dishes; place dishes in large baking dish. Add enough boiling water to come halfway up sides of small dishes.
3 Bake puddings 20 minutes, whisking gently with fork under the skin of the puddings twice – this stops the rice sinking to the bottom of the dishes. Sprinkle puddings with cinnamon; bake further 20 minutes or until set. Stand puddings 10 minutes before serving.

prep + cook time 1 hour **makes** 6

For the coconut rice puddings you will need to cook ⅓ cup (65g) white medium-grain rice for this recipe. Puddings can be stored, covered, in the refrigerator for up to 2 days.

apple turnovers

2 medium apples (300g), peeled, chopped finely
1 teaspoon caster sugar
2 tablespoons water
1 teaspoon pure icing sugar

gluten-free pastry
1¼ cups (225g) rice flour
¼ cup (35g) (corn) cornflour
¼ cup (30g) soya flour
⅓ cup (75g) caster sugar
150g cold butter, chopped coarsely
2 tablespoons cold water, approximately

This recipe is gluten-free, wheat-free and egg-free.

Stewed apple and pastry can be prepared up to two days ahead; keep covered, in the fridge. Turnovers can be made two days ahead, keep in an airtight container at room temperature. Turnovers are not suitable to freeze.

1 Preheat oven to 200°C/180°C fan-forced. Grease and line oven tray with baking paper.
2 Make gluten-free pastry.
3 Meanwhile, combine apple, sugar and the water in small saucepan; bring to the boil. Reduce heat; simmer, covered, about 5 minutes or until apple is tender. Cool.
4 Roll pastry between sheets of baking paper until 5mm thick; cut 18 x 8cm rounds from pastry. Drop heaped teaspoons of apple mixture into centre of each round; fold to enclose filling, pinching edges to seal. Place turnovers on tray.
5 Bake turnovers about 15 minutes; cool on trays. Serve dusted with sifted icing sugar.

gluten-free pastry Process flours, sugar and butter until crumbly. Add enough of the water to make ingredients come together. Knead dough lightly on floured surface until smooth.

prep + cook time 40 minutes **makes** 18

party food

The best day of the year for any kid is, of course, their birthday. There is so much excitement and anticipation for the children, and stress and nerves for the parents. Planning ahead is crucial. Make sure you nominate an end time to the party as well as the start time and that you have all the food ready or at least partially prepared beforehand. Finger food is easiest for everyone: you can put out big plates of it and the kids can reach in and serve themselves. Little fingers will get grubby so ensure there are plenty of napkins and paper towels about to wipe them, and the inevitable spillages, up. The food in this chapter is all so healthy and delicious that the kids won't even realise there's not a party pie in sight.

lamb kofta sticks

500g lamb mince
1 egg
1 small brown onion (80g), chopped finely
½ teaspoon ground cinnamon
1 tablespoon finely chopped fresh flat-leaf parsley
½ cup (140g) yogurt

1 Combine lamb, egg, onion, cinnamon and parsley in medium bowl.
2 Shape level tablespoons of lamb mixture into sausage shapes on 24 iceblock sticks; flatten slightly.
3 Cook kofta sticks, in batches, in heated oiled large frying pan until cooked through. Serve with yogurt.

prep + cook time 35 minutes **makes** 24

berry punch

250g strawberries
1 litre (4 cups) tropical fruit punch juice
1 litre (4 cups) chilled dry ginger ale
125g blueberries
125g raspberries
2 teaspoons grenadine

Grenadine is a non-alcoholic syrup made from pomegranate juice; bright red in colour, it's used to colour and flavour drinks and desserts. Grenadine-flavoured cordial is also available.

1 Finely chop half the strawberries; coarsely chop remaining strawberries.
2 Divide finely chopped strawberries into holes of 12-hole (1 tablespoon/20ml) ice-cube tray. Pour 1 cup of the juice into the holes; freeze 3 hours or overnight.
3 Combine remaining strawberries, remaining juice and strawberry ice cubes with remaining ingredients in large jug or punch bowl.

prep time 15 minutes (+ freezing) **makes** 2 litres (8 cups)

Kofta can be made and shaped onto the sticks a day ahead of the party; keep covered in the fridge. Uncooked kofta can be frozen for up to two months; thaw them in the fridge the night before the party.
You will need to soak 24 iceblock sticks in cold water for 1 hour to prevent scorching during cooking.

The bread stick can be prepared up to 12 hours before the party. Keep it wrapped and weighted in the fridge. Slice the stick as close to serving time as possible. Roasted zucchini, eggplant and capsicum can be bought loose from delis, making the job even easier.

toastie men

14 slices white bread (630g)
14 slices wholemeal bread (630g)
250g spreadable cream cheese
70g shaved ham, chopped finely
1 tablespoon finely chopped fresh chives
95g can tuna in springwater, drained
1 tablespoon finely chopped cornichons
1 tablespoon finely chopped fresh flat-leaf parsley

You can make toasts one day ahead and store in an airtight container. Make fillings one day ahead and store, covered, in the refrigerator. Assemble the toastie men several hours before the party.

1 Preheat grill.
2 Using gingerbread man cutter, cut three 5cm men from each slice of bread; place on oven trays. Toast bread, in batches, under grill until browned both sides.
3 Divide cream cheese into two small bowls; stir ham and chives into one bowl, and stir tuna, cornichons and parsley into remaining bowl.
4 Spread level teaspoons of ham mixture onto each white toast; spread level teaspoons of tuna mixture onto each wholemeal toast.

prep + cook time 45 minutes **makes** 42 of each

roasted vegie and ricotta bread

1 medium zucchini (120g), sliced thinly lengthways
1 small french bread stick (150g)
½ cup (120g) ricotta cheese
2 slices roasted eggplant (125g)
4 slices roasted red capsicum (170g)
½ cup (30g) finely shredded iceberg lettuce

1 Cook zucchini on heated oiled grill plate (or grill or barbecue) until tender. Cool.
2 Cut down centre of bread stick, without cutting all the way through. Open bread stick; remove soft bread inside, leaving 1cm-thick shell.
3 Spread cheese inside bread stick. Layer eggplant, capsicum, zucchini and lettuce inside bread case. Wrap bread stick tightly in plastic wrap.
4 Place bread stick on tray; top with another tray, weight with a small can. Refrigerate 3 hours before cutting.

prep + cook time 30 minutes (+ refrigeration) **makes** 16 slices

mini vegie burgers

12 small par-baked white dinner rolls (300g)
2 medium potatoes (400g), chopped coarsely
1 small carrot (70g), grated coarsely
1 medium tomato (150g), seeded, chopped finely
2 green onions, chopped finely
1 egg white
½ cup (50g) packaged breadcrumbs
⅓ cup (40g) coarsely grated cheddar cheese
1 cup (60g) finely shredded iceberg lettuce

barbecue sauce
¼ cup (60ml) tomato sauce
1 tablespoon cider vinegar
1 tablespoon brown sugar
2 teaspoons worcestershire sauce
2 teaspoons american-style mustard

Patties can be made a day before the party, keep them covered in the fridge. The sauce can be made a week before the party, keep covered in the fridge. Assemble the burgers up to 3 hours before the party.

1 Bake bread rolls following packet instructions.
2 Meanwhile, boil, steam or microwave potato until tender; drain. Push potato through sieve into medium bowl; stir in carrot, tomato, onion, egg white, breadcrumbs and cheese. Shape level tablespoons of mixture into 24 patties; place on baking-paper-lined tray. Cover, refrigerate 1 hour.
3 Meanwhile, make barbecue sauce.
4 Cook patties in heated oiled large frying pan until browned both sides.
5 Split rolls in half horizontally; cut each roll in half crossways. You will have 24 mini burger buns. Divide patties, lettuce and barbecue sauce between buns.

barbecue sauce Bring ingredients to the boil in small saucepan. Reduce heat; simmer, uncovered, stirring occasionally, about 10 minutes or until thickened.

prep + cook time 50 minutes (+ refrigeration) **makes** 24

chicken spring rolls

2 cups (500ml) water
200g chicken breast fillet
1 medium carrot (120g), grated coarsely
½ cup (40g) bean sprouts, chopped finely
1 tablespoon finely chopped fresh coriander
1 tablespoon light soy sauce
50 wonton wrappers

1 Bring the water to the boil in small saucepan; add chicken. Reduce heat; simmer, covered, about 10 minutes or until chicken is cooked through. Cool chicken in poaching liquid 10 minutes; drain, shred chicken finely using two forks.
2 Preheat oven to 220°C/200°C fan-forced. Grease and line oven tray with baking paper.
3 Combine chicken, carrot, sprouts, coriander and sauce in medium bowl.
4 Place rounded teaspoons of chicken mixture along bottom edge of each wrapper; fold in sides, moisten top edge with water, then roll up to enclose filling. Place on tray.
5 Bake spring rolls about 15 minutes or until rolls are browned and crisp.

prep + cook time 45 minutes **makes** 50

spaghetti bolognese baskets

150g angel hair spaghetti
1 egg
¼ cup (20g) finely grated parmesan cheese
2 teaspoons olive oil
1 stalk celery (150g), trimmed, chopped finely
1 small carrot (70g), chopped finely
1 small brown onion (80g), chopped finely
200g beef mince
1 tablespoon tomato paste
1 cup (260g) bottled tomato pasta sauce
36 small basil leaves

The pasta cases can be made, cooled and removed from the pans one day before the party. Store in an airtight container at room temperature. The bolognese sauce can be made two days ahead; keep it covered in the fridge. Assemble the baskets up to three hours before the party.

1 Preheat oven to 180°C/160°C fan-forced. Grease three 12-hole (1 tablespoon/20ml) round-based patty pans.
2 Cook pasta in large saucepan of boiling water until tender; drain. Cool.
3 Combine pasta, egg and cheese in medium bowl; divide pasta mixture into pan holes, press the mixture firmly to cover pan holes evenly.
4 Bake pasta baskets about 20 minutes or until set. Cool in pans.
5 Meanwhile, heat oil in medium frying pan. Cook vegetables, stirring, until soft. Add beef, cook, stirring, until browned. Add paste and sauce; bring to the boil. Reduce heat; simmer, uncovered, about 10 minutes or until bolognese thickens.
6 Remove pasta baskets from pan using metal spatula; transfer to serving plate. Divide bolognese into baskets; top each with a basil leaf.

prep + cook time 45 minutes **makes** 36

Serve with child-friendly sweet chilli or soy sauce for dipping, if you like. The rolls can be made a day before the party, keep covered with damp absorbent paper, then plastic wrap, in the fridge. Bake the rolls up to an hour before serving.

For the mushroom cups,
prepare the mushrooms, ready for grilling the day before the party, keep covered in the fridge. Mushrooms can be grilled up to 30 minutes before serving.

You will need 3 passionfruit
for the tropical jelly cups. The jelly cups can be made a day before the party; top with tropical salsa up to an hour before serving.

pesto mushroom cups

24 button mushrooms (300g)
½ cup (130g) bottled basil pesto
12 cherry tomatoes (100g), halved
½ cup (60g) coarsely grated cheddar cheese
24 small basil leaves

1 Remove stalks from mushrooms; place top-side down on foil-lined tray. Divide pesto into mushroom cups; top each with a tomato half, cut-side up, sprinkle with cheese.
2 Preheat grill.
3 Grill mushrooms about 5 minutes or until cheese melts. Serve each topped with a basil leaf.

prep + cook time 25 minutes **makes** 24

tropical jelly cups

1 tablespoon powdered gelatine
¼ cup (60ml) water
2¾ cups (680ml) tropical fruit juice
tropical salsa
1 medium banana (200g), chopped finely
½ medium mango (215g), chopped finely
¼ cup (60ml) passionfruit pulp

1 Sprinkle gelatine over the water in small heatproof jug; stand in small saucepan of simmering water, stirring, until gelatine dissolves.
2 Combine juice and gelatine mixture in large jug; pour ¼ cup (60ml) mixture into 12 x ½ cup (125ml) serving cups. Cover, refrigerate 3 hours or until set.
3 Meanwhile, make tropical salsa.
4 Just before serving, spoon level tablespoons of salsa into each cup.
tropical salsa Combine ingredients in a small bowl.

prep + cook time 20 minutes (+ refrigeration) **makes** 12

sticky chicken drummettes

¾ cup (180ml) tomato sauce
⅓ cup (80ml) plum sauce
2 tablespoons worcestershire sauce
1 tablespoon brown sugar
16 chicken drummettes (1kg)

Marinate the chicken up to a day before the party. Roast the chicken up to an hour before serving – don't forget to deal with the guests small sticky fingers.

1 Combine sauces and sugar in large bowl; add chicken. Cover; refrigerate 3 hours or overnight.
2 Preheat oven to 200°C/180°C fan-forced.
3 Drain chicken; discard marinade. Place chicken on oiled wire rack over large baking dish. Roast chicken about 30 minutes or until cooked through.

prep + cook time 40 minutes (+ refrigeration) **makes** 16

chicken and vegie rice paper rolls

1 large carrot (180g), grated coarsely
2 stalks celery (300g), trimmed, chopped finely
150g wombok, shredded finely
1½ cups (240g) finely shredded cooked chicken
½ cup (40g) bean sprouts, chopped coarsely
2 tablespoons lemon juice
1 tablespoon fish sauce
2 teaspoons brown sugar
24 x 17cm-square rice paper sheets
24 fresh mint leaves

1 Combine carrot, celery, wombok, chicken, sprouts, juice, sauce and sugar in medium bowl.
2 Place one sheet of rice paper in medium bowl of warm water until just softened. Lift sheet from water carefully; place on a tea-towel-covered board with a corner pointing towards you.
3 Place 1 rounded tablespoon of vegetable mixture horizontally in centre of sheet; top with one mint leaf. Fold corner facing you over filling; roll to cover filling, then fold in sides. Continue rolling to enclose filling. Repeat with remaining rice paper sheets, vegetable mixture and mint leaves.

prep time 35 minutes **makes** 24

Serve rice paper rolls with child friendly soy or sweet chilli sauce. Prepare the rolls up to 3 hours before the party; keep them on a tray, in a single layer, in the fridge, covered with a damp tea towel.

iceblocks

passionfruit and coconut ice-cream blocks

Place 1 cup softened vanilla ice-cream in small bowl; stir in ½ teaspoon coconut essence and 170g can passionfruit in syrup. Spoon mixture into six ¼-cup (60ml) iceblock moulds. Press lids on firmly; freeze 6 hours or overnight.

prep time 5 minutes (+ freezing)
makes 6

raspberry iceblocks

Heat 1 cup frozen raspberries and ⅓ cup icing sugar in small saucepan over low heat, stirring occasionally, about 5 minutes or until raspberries soften. Using back of large spoon, push raspberry mixture through sieve into medium jug; discard seeds. Stir 1 cup sparkling mineral water into jug. Pour mixture into six ¼-cup (60ml) iceblock moulds. Press lids on firmly; freeze 6 hours or overnight.

prep + cook time 15 minutes (+ freezing) **makes** 6

frozen fruit and yogurt blocks

Combine 1½ cups vanilla yogurt, 1 cup frozen mixed berries and 1 tablespoon honey in medium bowl; spoon into six ¼-cup (60ml) iceblock moulds. Press lids on firmly; freeze 6 hours or overnight.

prep time 10 minutes (+ freezing)
makes 6

pineapple and mint iceblocks

Combine 1½ cups pineapple juice, 2 tablespoons icing sugar mixture and 2 teaspoons finely chopped fresh mint in medium jug. Pour mixture into six ¼-cup (60ml) iceblock moulds. Press lids on firmly; freeze 6 hours or overnight.

prep time 5 minutes (+ freezing)
makes 6

orange and mango iceblocks

Strain 425g can sliced mango in natural juice over small bowl; reserve juice. Blend or process mango slices, ¼ cup of the reserved juice and ½ cup orange juice until smooth. Pour mixture into six ¼-cup (60ml) iceblock moulds. Press lids on firmly; freeze 6 hours or overnight.

prep time 5 minutes (+ freezing)
makes 6

polenta and avocado bites

3 cups (750ml) water
¾ cup (120g) polenta
½ cup (60g) coarsely grated cheddar cheese
1 medium avocado (250g)
2 teaspoons lemon juice
1 tablespoon olive oil
18 grape tomatoes (145g), halved

1 Oil deep 20cm-square cake pan.
2 Place the water in medium saucepan; bring to the boil. Gradually stir polenta into the water; reduce heat. Simmer, stirring, about 10 minutes or until polenta thickens. Stir in cheese; spread polenta into pan, cool 10 minutes. Cover; refrigerate 1 hour or until polenta is firm.
3 Meanwhile, mash avocado and juice in small bowl, until almost smooth.
4 Turn polenta onto board; cut polenta into 36 squares. Heat oil in large frying pan; cook polenta, turning, until browned all over.
5 Top polenta squares with avocado mixture, then tomatoes.

prep + cook time 35 minutes (+ refrigeration) **makes** 36

fruity rockets

2 small apples (260g)
2 medium kiwifruit (170g), peeled
1 large orange (300g), peeled
1 small banana (130g)
6 small strawberries (90g), hulled

The apples and banana will need to be cut as close to serving as possible, as they discolour quite fast once they're cut. If you like, you can sprinkle cut banana and apple with lemon juice to help present discolouration.

1 Remove cores carefully from apples, keeping the hole as small and neat as possible. Cut each apple and kiwifruit crossways into three slices. Cut a 5.5cm circle from each apple slice. Cut orange and banana crossways into six slices.
2 Place orange slices on serving plates; top each with an apple round. Push a toothpick into the centre of each orange and apple stack. Thread a slice of kiwifruit, banana and then strawberry onto each stack.

prep time 15 minutes **makes** 6

Toothpicks can be a hazard for young children; serve the fruity rockets to older children only, and keep an eye on them while they enjoy it. The orange, kiwifruit and strawberries can be prepared, ready for stacking up to 3 hours ahead of the party.

You could omit the green onions from the rissoles and replace them with ¼ cup finely chopped fresh flat-leaf parsley.

Serve tomato or barbecue sauce with the chicken and vegetable rolls.

mini beef rissoles

1kg lean beef mince
1 cup (70g) stale breadcrumbs
½ cup (40g) coarsely grated parmesan cheese
2 cloves garlic, crushed
2 green onions, sliced thinly
1 tablespoon worcestershire sauce
2 tablespoons barbecue sauce
1 tablespoon olive oil

1 Using hand, combine beef, breadcrumbs, cheese, garlic, onion and sauces in large bowl; shape rounded tablespoons of the mixture into rissoles.
2 Heat oil in large non-stick frying pan; cook rissoles, in batches, until cooked through. Drain on absorbent paper.
3 Serve rissoles with tomato sauce.

prep + cook time 45 minutes **makes** 30

chicken and vegetable rolls

500g chicken mince
1 clove garlic, crushed
1 medium brown onion (150g), chopped finely
1 medium carrot (120g), chopped finely
100g green beans, trimmed, chopped finely
125g can creamed corn
1 egg, beaten lightly
⅓ cup (25g) stale breadcrumbs
1 tablespoon tomato sauce
3 sheets ready-rolled puff pastry
1 egg, beaten lightly, extra

1 Preheat oven to 200°C/180°C fan-forced. Oil two oven trays.
2 Using hand, combine mince, garlic, onion, carrot, beans, corn, egg, breadcrumbs and sauce in large bowl.
3 Cut pastry sheets in half lengthways. Place equal amounts of chicken mixture lengthways along centre of each pastry piece; roll each pastry piece, from one wide edge, to enclose filling. Cut each roll into six pieces. Place, seam-side down, on trays; brush with extra egg.
4 Bake rolls about 30 minutes or until browned lightly and cooked through.

prep + cook time 45 minutes **makes** 36

aussie pizzas

1 rindless bacon rasher (65g), sliced thinly
1 egg, beaten lightly
⅓ cup (35g) coarsely grated pizza cheese
30cm (300g) frozen ready-made pizza base, thawed
2 tablespoons bottled tomato pasta sauce

1 Preheat oven to 200°C/180°C fan-forced.
2 Heat small frying pan; cook bacon, stirring, until crisp. Add egg; cook, stirring, until egg just sets. Remove from heat; stir in cheese.
3 Using 5cm Australia-shape cutter, cut shapes from pizza base; place bases on oven trays.
4 Spread sauce on bases; top with bacon mixture. Bake 10 minutes or until brown and crisp.

prep + cook time 35 minutes **makes** 15

barbecue pizzas

30cm (300g) frozen ready-made pizza base, thawed
2 tablespoons barbecue sauce
½ cup (80g) finely shredded barbecued chicken
⅓ cup (40g) coarsely grated cheddar cheese

1 Preheat oven to 200°C/180°C fan-forced.
2 Using 5cm-square cutter, cut shapes from pizza base; place bases on oven trays.
3 Spread sauce on bases; top with chicken and cheese. Bake 10 minutes or until brown and crisp.

prep + cook time 30 minutes **makes** 15

vegetarian pizzas

30cm (300g) frozen ready-made pizza base, thawed
2 tablespoons tomato paste
⅓ cup (40g) seeded green olives, chopped finely
2 tablespoons finely chopped green capsicum
2 tablespoons finely chopped red capsicum
120g baby bocconcini, chopped finely

1 Preheat oven to 200°C/180°C fan-forced.
2 Using 5cm heart-shape cutter, cut shapes from pizza base; place bases on oven trays.
3 Spread paste on bases. Combine olives, capsicums and cheese in small bowl; top pizzas with olive mixture. Bake about 10 minutes or until brown and crisp.

prep + cook time 30 minutes **makes** 15

aussie pizzas

Jack and Jill

Jack and Jill went up the hill
To fetch a pail of water;
Jack fell down and broke his crown,
And Jill came tumbling after.

barbecue pizzas

vegetarian pizzas

chicken and creamed corn sandwiches

salami, mushroom and cheese pizzas

Georgie Porgie

Georgie Porgie, pudding and pie,
Kissed the girls and made them cry;
When the boys came out to play,
Georgie Porgie ran away.

tuna and carrot pinwheels

chicken and creamed corn sandwiches

1¼ cups (200g) finely chopped cooked chicken
125g can creamed corn
8 slices wholemeal bread
2 tablespoons mayonnaise
1 cup (60g) coarsely shredded iceberg lettuce

1 Combine chicken and corn in medium bowl.
2 Spread four slices of the bread with mayonnaise; top with chicken mixture and lettuce then remaining bread slices. Discard crusts; cut sandwiches into fingers.

prep time 10 minutes **makes** 12

salami, mushroom and cheese pizzas

30cm (300g) frozen ready-made pizza base, thawed
2 tablespoons bottled tomato pasta sauce
10 slices salami (150g), sliced thinly
5 button mushrooms (60g), sliced thickly
5 slices swiss cheese (100g), sliced thinly

1 Preheat oven to 200°C/180°C fan-forced.
2 Using 5cm-round cutter, cut shapes from pizza base; place bases on oven trays.
3 Spread sauce on bases; top with salami, mushrooms and cheese. Bake about 10 minutes or until brown and crisp.

prep + cook time 30 minutes **makes** 15

tuna and carrot pinwheels

185g can tuna in brine, drained
1 small carrot (70g), grated finely
2 gherkins (40g), chopped finely
¼ cup (75g) mayonnaise
6 slices lavash
2 tablespoons mayonnaise, extra

1 Combine tuna, carrot, gherkins and mayonnaise in medium bowl.
2 Spread one slice of bread with ⅓ of the extra mayonnaise; top with another piece of bread. Spread ⅓ of the tuna mixture along short edge of bread. Roll bread tightly; trim edges. Using serrated knife, cut roll into four pieces.
3 Repeat with remaining bread, extra mayonnaise and tuna mixture.

prep time 20 minutes **makes** 12

cheesy pastry twists

2 sheets puff pastry, thawed
1 egg yolk, beaten
1 cup (100g) coarsely grated pizza cheese
½ cup (40g) finely grated parmesan cheese

1 Preheat oven to 200°C/180°C fan-forced. Oil two oven trays; line with baking paper.
2 Brush one pastry sheet with half of the egg yolk; sprinkle with pizza cheese. Top with remaining pastry sheet; brush with remaining egg yolk. Sprinkle with parmesan cheese. Cut pastry stack in half; place one pastry half on top of the other, pressing down firmly to seal.
3 Cut pastry widthways into 24 strips; twist each, pinching ends to seal. Place twists on trays; bake about 10 minutes or until browned lightly.

prep + cook time 30 minutes **makes** 24

mini chocolate brownie triangles

125g butter, chopped
200g dark eating chocolate, chopped coarsely
¾ cup (165g) caster sugar
1 teaspoon vanilla extract
2 eggs, beaten lightly
1 cup (150g) plain flour

1 Preheat oven to 180°C/160°C fan-forced. Grease deep 19cm-square cake pan; line base and two sides with baking paper, extending paper 2cm above edges of pan.
2 Stir butter and chocolate in medium heatproof bowl over medium saucepan of simmering water until smooth. Remove from heat; stir in sugar and extract then eggs and flour. Pour mixture into pan; bake about 30 minutes or until just firm. Cool in pan.
3 Turn brownie onto board; cut into 16 squares then halve squares to form triangles.

prep + cook time 50 minutes (+ standing) **makes** 32

The cheesy pastry twists can be cut and twisted into any shape you like.

For an easy sour cream frosting, melt 100g dark eating chocolate and fold it into ¼ cup sour cream.

You will need 12 iceblock sticks to make the teddy bear biscuits.

When making the chocolate crackles, you'll need to work quite quickly when dividing the mixture among the muffin holes, as the chocolate sets quickly.

teddy bear biscuits

200g butter, softened
1 teaspoon vanilla extract
¾ cup (165g) caster sugar
1 egg
40g dark eating chocolate, grated finely
1¼ cups (175g) plain flour
2 tablespoons cocoa powder
24 mini M&M's
12 dark chocolate Melts

1 Preheat oven to 180°C/160°C fan-forced. Grease three oven trays; line with baking paper.
2 Beat butter, extract, sugar and egg in small bowl with electric mixer until just changed to a pale colour; do not overbeat. Stir in chocolate, sifted flour and cocoa. Refrigerate 15 minutes.
3 Roll 24 level teaspoons of the mixture into balls. Roll remaining mixture into 12 large balls for teddy faces. On each tray, flatten four large balls with palm of hand to form an 8cm diameter circle. Position two small balls on top of each circle for ears. Flatten balls with palm of hand. Slide one iceblock stick two-thirds of the way into dough on each face.
4 Position M&M's into dough for eyes and Melts for nose.
5 Bake biscuits about 12 minutes or until browned lightly. Cool on trays.

prep + cook time 50 minutes (+ refrigeration) **makes** 12

white chocolate crackles

1 cup (35g) Rice Bubbles
1 cup (35g) Coco Pops
2 x 35g tubes mini M&M's
1 cup (200g) white chocolate Melts, melted

1 Line two 12-hole (1 tablespoon/20ml) mini muffin pans with patty-pan cases.
2 Combine ingredients in medium bowl.
3 Divide mixture into cases; cover, refrigerate 10 minutes.

prep time 10 minutes (+ refrigeration) **makes** 24

party cakes

This chapter has wonderful cake recipes that are sure to delight your child on his most important day of the year. Birthday cakes can be works of art, but must also be safe for your little one and all his friends. Make sure you don't use anything sharp to hold parts of the cake together, such as toothpicks or skewers. Lollies are fabulous decorations but if the children are under two they can easily get lodged in their throats and are a choking hazard.

Also important is to have the cake ready well before the party kicks off. The last thing you want to be doing is frantically getting the finishing touches done as guests arrive.

one

equipment
12-hole (⅓-cup/80ml) standard muffin pan
6 standard paper cases (blue)
3.5cm- and 6.5cm-wide duck-shaped cutters
new clean small paint brush
20cm x 50cm prepared cake board (see page 280)

cake
½ x 470g packet buttercake mix
½ quantity butter cream (see page 280)
blue food colouring

decorations
¼ cup (40g) icing sugar
100g ready-made white icing (see page 280)
yellow and orange food colouring
6 blue rainbow choc-chips

1 Preheat oven to 180°C/160°C fan-forced. Line muffin pan with the paper cases.

2 Make cake according to directions on packet. Drop 2½ level tablespoons of the mixture into each paper case; bake about 20 minutes. Stand cakes in pan 5 minutes; turn, top-side up, onto wire rack to cool.

3 On a surface dusted with sifted icing sugar, knead the ready-made icing until smooth; tint with yellow colouring. Roll icing until 3mm thick; using cutters, cut two large ducks and five small ducks from the icing. Brush one side of a large duck sparingly, but evenly, with water. Gently press the other large duck onto the wet surface.

4 Using the paint brush, paint an orange beak on each side of the mother duck's head. Gently press blue rainbow choc-chips into the icing to make the eyes. Lay mother duck flat on a baking-paper-lined tray to dry. Paint beaks and position eyes on ducklings; dry on tray with mother duck.

5 Tint butter cream blue; spread over tops of cakes. Position cakes on prepared board to resemble the number 1; secure with a little butter cream.

6 Using picture as a guide, position mother duck and ducklings on cakes.

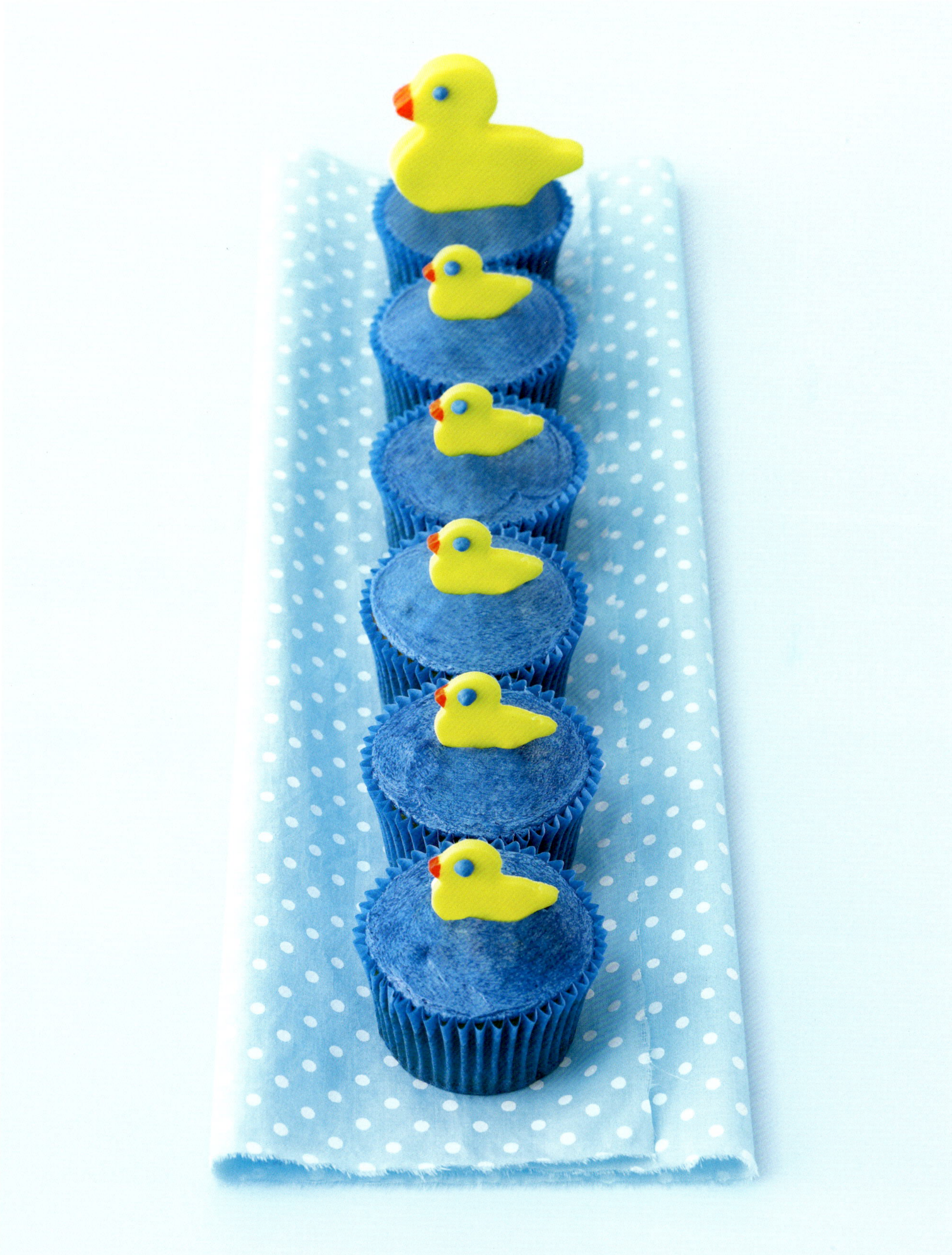

two

equipment
12-hole (⅓-cup/80ml) standard muffin pan
12 standard paper cases (6 green, 6 brown)
30cm x 45cm prepared cake board (see page 280)

cake
470g packet buttercake mix
½ quantity butter cream (see page 280)
green food colouring
3 teaspoons cocoa powder

decorations
black and red decorating gel
6 banana lollies
6 brown rainbow choc-chips
1 x 30cm (3mm) brown chenille stick (pipe cleaner)
edible silver glitter
3 sour worms
35g tube mini M&M's
7 mint leaves

We set this cake up on artificial grass instead of a board. To create a wonderful world for an insect-themed party, cover the party table with the grass and decorate the table with different types of plastic insects.

1 Preheat oven to 180°C/160°C fan-forced. Line muffin pan with the paper cases.

2 Make cake according to directions on packet. Drop 2½ level tablespoons of the mixture into each paper case; bake about 20 minutes. Stand cakes in pan 5 minutes; turn, top-side up, onto wire rack to cool.

3 Tint half the butter cream green. Divide remaining butter cream into two small bowls. Stir 2 teaspoons of the sifted cocoa into one bowl; stir remaining sifted cocoa into remaining butter cream.

4 Using the cakes in the brown paper cases, spread the dark brown butter cream over three cakes; spread the light brown butter cream over three cakes.

5 Using picture as a guide, use the black decorating gel to draw spirals on the brown cakes for snails' shells. Position bananas for bodies. Use the red decorating gel to pipe mouths on the snails. Secure the rainbow choc-chips for eyes with a little butter cream. Cut the chenille stick into 12 x 2.5cm pieces; position in cakes for feelers.

6 Using picture as a guide, spread green butter cream over remaining cakes. Sprinkle glitter carefully over each cake to make snails' trails. Using the handle of a teaspoon, make a small hole in three of the cakes; gently push worms into position. Decorate cakes with mini M&M's and mint leaves.

7 Assemble cakes on prepared board in the shape of the number 2. Secure with a little butter cream.

three

equipment

12-hole (⅓-cup/80ml) standard muffin pan
11 standard paper cases
1.5cm-round cutter
35cm x 45cm prepared cake board (see page 280)

cake

470g packet buttercake mix
1 quantity butter cream (see page 280)
yellow and pink food colouring

decorations

¼ cup (40g) icing sugar
60g ready-made white icing (see page 280)
2 large pink marshmallows, halved
5 large white marshmallows, halved
35g tube mini M&M's
3 pink Mallow Bakes, halved
1 white Mallow Bake, halved
1m length black licorice bootlace

Three year olds love nursery rhymes, and even though the mice are clearly not blind – they're having fun finding the cheese. You'll have 1 cup of the cake mixture left over; use it to make more cakes for your guests. We used the mouse traps as a prop in the photo; it's best not to use them at a children's party because of safety concerns.

1 Preheat oven to 180°C/160°C fan-forced. Line muffin pan with the paper cases.

2 Make cake according to directions on packet. Drop 2½ level tablespoons of the mixture into each paper case; bake about 20 minutes. Stand cakes in pan 5 minutes; turn, top-side up, onto wire rack to cool.

3 Divide butter cream into four small bowls. Tint one bowl yellow, tint remaining bowls various shades of pink (light, medium, dark).

4 Spread yellow butter cream over four cakes. Using picture as a guide, spread pink butter cream over remaining seven cakes.

5 On a surface dusted with sifted icing sugar, knead the ready-made icing until smooth; tint yellow (see page 280). Roll icing until 3mm thick. Cut out 2 x 5cm squares. Cut a few 1.5cm rounds from the squares to give the look of swiss cheese; cut each square into two triangles. Position cheese triangles on yellow cakes.

6 Using picture as a guide, position marshmallow halves for ears and mini M&M's for eyes. Position Mallow Bake halves for noses. Cut 28 x 1cm pieces from licorice bootlace; use these to make whiskers. Position cakes on prepared board to resemble the number 3; secure with a little butter cream. Cut 7 x 10cm pieces from licorice bootlace to make tails; push into cakes.

ROMAK

four

equipment
12-hole (⅓-cup/80ml) standard muffin pan
9 standard paper cases (blue)
4.5cm-round cutter
fluted pastry wheel
30cm x 45cm prepared cake board
(see page 280)

cake
470g packet buttercake mix
½ quantity butter cream (see page 280)
blue, pink and yellow food colouring

decorations
½ cup (80g) icing sugar
200g ready-made white icing
(see page 280)
yellow, green and pink food colouring
2 red mini M&M's
hundreds and thousands
60g jar mixed cachous

A cupcake on a cupcake is going to delight girls of any age. They're not difficult to make, but it will take a little time to make the cupcake shapes.

1 Preheat oven to 180°C/160°C fan-forced. Line muffin pan with the paper cases.

2 Make cake according to directions on packet. Drop 2½ level tablespoons of the mixture into each paper case; bake about 20 minutes. Stand cakes in pan 5 minutes; turn, top-side up, onto wire rack to cool.

3 Divide butter cream equally into three small bowls; tint each bowl with one of the suggested colours: blue, pink and yellow. Spread blue butter cream over three cakes, pink butter cream over two cakes and yellow butter cream over four cakes.

4 On a surface dusted with sifted icing sugar, knead the ready-made icing until smooth. Divide icing into three equal portions; tint each portion with one of the suggested colours: yellow, green and pink. Roll each portion until 3mm thick.

5 Cut two 4.5cm rounds from the yellow icing; cut three 4.5cm rounds from the green icing; cut four 4.5cm rounds from the pink icing. Cut each round in half for the cupcake "tops". Using picture as a guide, position "tops" on cakes.

6 Working with one icing portion at a time, use a fluted pastry wheel to cut a 3cm x 18cm strip from yellow, green and pink icings. Cut two yellow, three pink and four green patty case "bases" from each strip of icing. Mark vertical lines on each of the "bases". Position "bases" on cakes.

7 Brush a tiny amount of water onto tops of the cupcake "tops" and "bases"; decorate with mini M&M's, hundreds and thousands and cachous.

8 Position cakes on prepared board to resemble the number 4; secure with a little butter cream.

five

equipment
12-hole (⅓-cup/80ml) standard muffin pan
11 standard paper cases (orange)
35cm x 45cm prepared cake board (see page 280)

cake
470g packet buttercake mix
½ quantity butter cream (see page 280)
orange and pink food colouring

decorations
4 x 35g tubes mini M&M's
3 small pink jelly beans, halved crossways
1 musk stick, cut into thin strips
1 red sour strap, cut into 10 x 2cm strips
10 large pink candy hearts

You'll have about 1 cup of the cake mixture left over; use to make extra cakes for the party.

1 Preheat oven to 180°C/160°C fan-forced. Line muffin pan with the paper cases.
2 Make cake according to directions on packet. Drop 2½ level tablespoons of the mixture into each paper case; bake about 20 minutes. Stand cakes in pan 5 minutes; turn, top-side up, onto wire rack to cool.
3 Divide butter cream into two small bowls; tint one bowl of butter cream orange, tint the other bowl pink. Spread orange butter cream over the tops of five cakes; spread pink butter cream over the remaining six cakes.
4 Using picture as a guide, assemble cakes on the prepared board in the shape of the number 5; secure with a little butter cream. Decorate each pink cake using orange mini M&M's to make heart shapes.
5 Decorate the five remaining kitty face cakes using the pink mini M&M's for eyes and jelly bean halves for the noses. Cut the musk stick strips into 20 x 2.5cm lengths; use for whiskers. Shape and position two lengths of the sour strap strips for mouths. Use the hearts to make the ears for each kitty.

up, up and away...

equipment
3 deep 20cm-round cake pans
52cm-round prepared board (see page 280)

cake
3 x 340g packets buttercake mix
½ cup (160g) apricot jam, warmed, sieved

decorations
icing sugar
pink, green and blue colouring
2.5kg ready-made soft icing (see page 280)
1m (2cm-wide) blue ribbon
1m (2cm-wide) pink ribbon
1m (2cm-wide) green ribbon

1 Preheat oven to 180°C/160°C fan-forced. Grease and line cake pans.

2 Make cake according to directions on packet. Divide mixture into pans; bake about 40 minutes. Stand cakes in pans 5 minutes; turn onto wire racks to cool.

3 Using small serrated knife, trim cake tops to make more rounded, as shown. Brush jam all over cakes.

4 On surface dusted with icing sugar, knead icing until smooth; knead pink colouring into ⅓ of the icing. Reserve a walnut-sized amount for balloon end; enclose in plastic wrap.

5 Using rolling pin, roll remaining pink icing into circle large enough to cover one cake. Using rolling pin, lift icing over one cake; using sharp-pointed knife, neatly trim excess icing. Position cake on board.

6 Using hands dusted with icing sugar, gently mould icing into balloon shape.

7 On surface dusted with icing sugar, make balloon end from reserved pink icing. Using toothpick or skewer, make creases in balloon end. Using toothpick, push end of ribbon into balloon end; attach to cake with a tiny dab of water.

8 Repeat with remaining cakes, icing, colourings and ribbons.

Using a small serrated knife, trim the tops of the cakes to make more rounded.

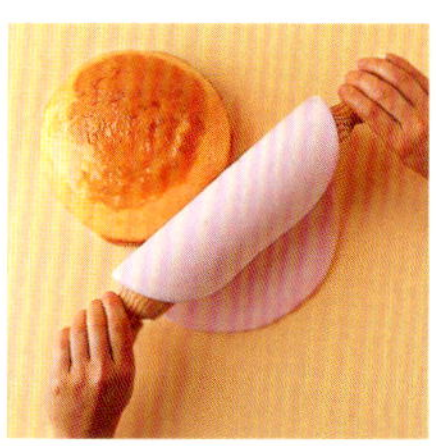
When icing is large enough to cover the cake, carefully lift icing over cake using a rolling pin.

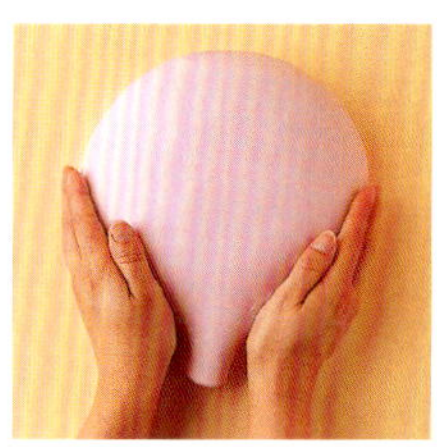
Dust your hands with icing sugar then gently mould the icing into a balloon shape.

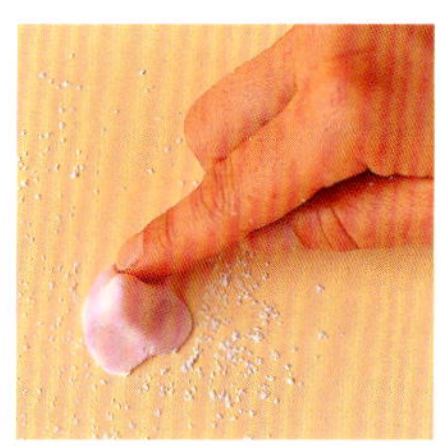
On a surface dusted with icing sugar, mould the balloon end from the reserved icing.

Using a toothpick or skewer, make small creases in the underside of the balloon end.

express train

equipment

deep 23cm-square care pan
22cm x 37cm prepared board
(see page 280)

cake

2 x 340g packets buttercake mix
400g jam roll
2 quantities butter cream (see page 280)
green colouring

decorations

2 red licorice straps
8 Carnival Pops
1 red Super Rope licorice
2 giant green Smarties
1 large yellow Sour Ball
22 yellow Smarties
8 red Smarties
1 Screw Pop
artificial spider's web

When it comes to eating this cake, remember that a small segment of stick is still embedded in each Carnival Pop (used for wheels).

1 Preheat oven to 180°C/160°C fan-forced. Grease and line cake pan.
2 Make cake according to directions on packet, pour into pan; bake about 1 hour. Stand cake in pan 5 minutes; turn onto wire rack to cool.
3 Using serrated knife, level cake top. Cut square cake in half; cut 2.5cm piece from one half of square cake. Cut 3.5cm piece from jam roll. Assemble cakes on board to form train, as shown; discard remaining cake.
4 Tint butter cream with green colouring; spread all over train.
5 Cut licorice strap into thin strips; using licorice, outline train's edges and make window on train.
6 Trim and discard sticks from Carnival Pops; position as wheels. Cut eight 1.5cm pieces from Super Rope; position between wheels as axle.
7 Cut two 8cm pieces from Super Rope; position at front of train for bumper. Position giant Smarties and Sour Ball at front of train for lights. Decorate train with yellow and red Smarties.
8 Place Screw Pop in position for funnel; place a little of the butter cream on top of funnel. Press the end of a piece of spider's web into the butter cream for smoke.

Cut a 2.5cm piece from one half of the square cake and trim a 3.5cm piece from the jam roll.

Assemble the cakes on the board to form the train; discard any remaining cake and jam roll.

pinky bunny

equipment
9-hole (½-cup/125ml) friand pan
8-hole (½-cup/125ml) mini loaf pan
25cm-square prepared cake board (see page 280)

cake
½ x 470g packet buttercake mix
½ quantity butter cream (see page 280)
pink food colouring

decorations
1 pink Mallow Bake
1 strip black licorice bootlace
2 brown M&M's
3 red mini M&M's
14 white Mallow Bakes
1 diamond-shaped red jube
1 giant white marshmallow

Pinky bunny is a small cute cake – just enough for a small cute person's birthday. You'll have ½ cup of the cake mixture left over, enough for another mini loaf.

1 Preheat oven to 170°C/150°C fan-forced. Grease three holes of the friand pan; grease one hole of the mini loaf pan.
2 Make cake according to directions on packet. Drop 2½ level tablespoons of the mixture into the greased holes of the friand pan. Drop ⅓ cup of the mixture into the greased hole of the mini loaf pan. Bake cakes about 20 minutes. Stand cakes in pans 5 minutes; turn, top-side up, onto wire rack to cool.
3 Level cake tops so they are the same height. Trim corners from the loaf cake to make an oval shape for the bunny's body.
4 Tint butter cream pink; spread over tops and sides of cakes. Using picture as a guide, position cakes on board; secure with a little butter cream.
5 Cut the pink Mallow Bake in half, trim into triangular shape for nose; position on cake. Cut 4 x 2cm pieces bootlace for whiskers and 2 x 3cm pieces for mouth; position on cake. Position brown M&M's for eyes and red M&M's for buttons. Position white Mallow Bakes on bunny's ears.
6 Split jube in half lengthways; trim to make bow tie. Use giant marshmallow for bunny's tail; secure to board with a little butter cream.

butterfly cakes

equipment

3 x 12-hole (⅓-cup/80ml) standard muffin pans
30 standard paper cases

cake

2 x 470g packets buttercake mix
3¼ cups (500g) icing sugar
2 tablespoons water, approximately
pink and green food colouring
1 cup (80g) desiccated coconut
600ml thickened cream
2 tablespoons icing sugar, extra
⅓ cup (110g) strawberry jam

decorations

15 small pink jelly beans
15 pink ready-made icing flowers

A tiered cake plate is the perfect way to show off these ever-popular patty cakes. Make sure you have enough cakes for your guests.

1 Preheat oven to 180°C/160°C fan-forced. Line muffin pans with the paper cases.
2 Make cake according to directions on packets. Drop 2½ level tablespoons of the mixture into each paper case; bake about 20 minutes. Stand cakes in pans 5 minutes; turn, top-side up, onto wire rack to cool.
3 Sift half the icing sugar into a medium heatproof bowl; stir in enough water to make a stiff paste. Place bowl over medium saucepan of simmering water (do not let the water touch the bottom of the bowl); stir until icing is thin and spreadable. Tint with pink colouring.
4 Place coconut in a shallow bowl. Spread (or dip) the tops of half the cakes with icing; dip tops in coconut, stand cakes on wire rack to set.
5 Repeat step 3 with remaining icing sugar and water; tint with green colouring. Spread (or dip) the tops of remaining cakes with icing; dip tops in coconut, stand cakes on wire rack to set.
6 Meanwhile, beat cream and extra sifted icing sugar in small bowl with electric mixer until soft peaks form.
7 Cut 5mm-thick rounds from tops of all the cakes. Cut pink rounds in half to form butterfly "wings"; leave green rounds whole.
8 Drop ½ teaspoon jam into the hole in each cake; dollop with cream. Using picture as a guide, position "wings" on the pink cakes; top with jelly beans. Top green cakes with green rounds; secure flowers to cakes with a little cream.

bush buddies

equipment
6-hole (¾-cup/180ml) texas muffin pan
1 texas muffin paper case

cake
470g packet buttercake mix
½ quantity fluffy frosting (see page 280)
½ quantity butter cream (see page 280)
black and brown food colouring

decorations
koala
1 Milk Arrowroot biscuit, halved crossways
1 white marshmallow, halved crossways
2 blue mini M&M's
1 small solid milk chocolate egg
3cm piece licorice strap, cut into a thin strip

cockatoo
2 brown mini M&M's
1 triangular black jube, halved crossways
6 banana lollies

echidna
2 yellow mini M&M's
12 thin mint sticks, halved
1 chocolate malt stick, halved

wombat
2 green mini M&M's
1 clinker, halved crossways
5cm piece black licorice strap

These cakes would work well for an Australian-themed outback party; maybe make one bush buddy for each guest. The cockatoo and koala will lose their gloss after an hour or so as the frosting sets like a meringue. You will have a small amount of cake mixture left over – barely enough for one more cake.

1 Preheat oven to 180°C/160°C fan-forced. Line one hole of the texas muffin pan with the paper case; grease three pan holes.

2 Make cake according to directions on packet. Pour ⅓ cup of the mixture into the paper case and greased pan holes; bake about 25 minutes. Stand cakes in pan 5 minutes; turn, top-side up, onto wire rack to cool.

3 Transfer half the fluffy frosting to a small bowl; use black colouring to tint frosting grey. Leave remaining frosting white. Tint the butter cream brown.

koala Shape biscuit halves into rounded shapes for ears. Spread grey frosting over top of cake in paper case and over top and edges of both ears. Using picture as a guide, position ears on cake; top ears with marshmallow halves. Position remaining decorations to make koala's eyes, nose and mouth.

cockatoo Level one cake top; turn cake cut-side down. Trim cake into a rounded oval shape. Spread white frosting over the cake. Using picture as a guide, decorate cake using the lollies for the cockatoo.

echidna Level one cake top; turn cake cut-side down. Trim cake into a tear-drop shape. Spread brown butter cream over the cake. Using picture as a guide, decorate cake using the lollies for the echidna.

wombat Level one cake top; turn cake cut-side down. Trim cake into a rounded oval shape. Spread brown butter cream over the cake. Using picture as a guide, decorate cake using the lollies for the wombat. Use a fork to mark frosting for a "furry" look.

cake basics

preparing cake boards

Use foil or other grease-repelling paper for covering cake boards. For round and oval boards, trace around the board on the back of the paper, cut the paper about 2cm outside the traced line. Snip the paper, almost up to the traced line, then fold and paste the snipped edges onto the board. Square boards are quicker and easier to cover. Trace the shape of the board on the back of the paper; cut the paper 2cm outside the traced line. Neatly fold the corners over and paste (or tape) to the back of the board. Boards can be made from craft wood, Masonite, or heavy card, or can be bought, already covered, from cake decorating supply shops.

icing recipes

butter cream

Basic butter cream is also known as vienna cream; the flavour can be varied by adding any essence you like.

125g butter, softened
1½ cups (240g) icing sugar
2 tablespoons milk

1 Beat butter in small bowl with electric mixer until as white as possible.
2 Gradually beat in half the sifted sugar, milk, then remaining sugar.
Chocolate variation Sift ⅓ cup (35g) cocoa powder in with the first batch of icing sugar.

fluffy frosting

1 cup (220g) caster sugar
⅓ cup (80ml) water
2 egg whites

1 Combine sugar and the water in small saucepan; stir with a wooden spoon over high heat, without boiling, until sugar dissolves. Boil, uncovered, without stirring, about 3 to 5 minutes or until syrup is slightly thick. If a candy thermometer is available, the syrup will be ready when it reaches 114°C (240°F).
2 When the syrup is thick, remove the pan from the heat, allow the bubbles to subside then test the syrup by dropping 1 teaspoon into a cup of cold water. The syrup should form a ball of soft sticky toffee. The syrup should not be changed in colour; if it has, it has been cooked for too long and you will have to discard it and start again.
3 While the syrup is boiling (see step 1), and after about four minutes, beat the egg whites in a small bowl with an electric mixer until stiff; keep beating (or the whites will deflate) until syrup reaches the correct temperature.
4 When syrup is ready, allow bubbles to subside then pour a very thin stream onto the egg whites with mixer operating on medium speed. If the syrup is added too quickly to the egg whites the frosting will not thicken.
5 Continue beating and adding syrup until all syrup is used. Continue to beat until frosting stands in stiff peaks (frosting should be barely warm).
6 For best results, frosting should be applied to a cake on the day it is to be served. While you can frost the cake the day before, the frosting will become crisp and lose its glossy appearance, much like a meringue.

ready-made white icing

This is available from cake-decorating suppliers and some health-food shops, delicatessens and supermarkets. There are several brands available, and they can be sold as Soft Icing, Prepared Icing or Ready-to-Roll Icing. This is very easy to use. Break off as much icing as you need; re-wrap remaining icing to exclude the air, or a crust will develop, which will spoil the smooth texture of the icing.
Knead the piece of icing on a surface lightly dusted with sifted icing sugar. If colouring the icing, start working tiny amounts of the colouring through the icing. The icing should be smooth and free from stickiness. Only work with small amounts of icing at the one time as the air will dry it out. Cover any rolled-out icing with plastic wrap.

glossary

ALLSPICE also called pimento; available whole or ground.

BAKING POWDER a raising agent; also available as gluten-free.

BARLEY a nutritious grain used in soups and stews. Hulled barley (the least processed), is high in fibre. Pearl barley has had the husk removed then hulled and polished so that only the "pearl" of the original grain remains.

BEANS
butter also called lima beans; large, flat, kidney-shaped bean, off-white in colour, with a mealy texture and mild taste. Available canned and dried.
mexe-style (mexican-style) a mildly-spiced canned combination of kidney or pinto beans, capsicum and tomato.

BICARBONATE OF SODA also called baking or carb soda; a leavening agent.

BREAD
french stick has been formed into a long, narrow cylindrical loaf. Also called french bread, french loaf or baguette.
fruit loaf contains sultanas and other dried fruits and spices.
par-baked partially-baked bread only needing a few minutes in the oven to give fresh-baked rolls. Available from most supermarkets.
pitta also known as lebanese bread. Sold in large, flat pieces that separate into two thin rounds. Also available in small thick pieces called pocket pitta.
turkish also known as pide; comes in long (about 45cm) flat loaves as well as individual rounds.

BROCCOLINI a cross between broccoli and chinese kale; its long asparagus-like stems and long loose floret, are edible.

BUK CHOY, BABY also known as pak kat farang or shanghai bok choy, is much smaller and more tender than buk choy.

BURGHUL also called bulghur wheat; it is not the same as cracked wheat.

CAPERS the grey-green buds of a warm climate (usually Mediterranean) shrub; sold dried and salted, or pickled in brine.

CAPSICUM also called bell pepper.
roasted available loose from delis or packed in jars in oil or brine.

CHEESE
bocconcini a walnut-sized, baby mozzarella. A delicate, semi-soft, white cheese; spoils rapidly so refrigerate in brine, for 2 days at most.
fetta Greek in origin; a sharp, salty, crumbly goat- or sheep-milk cheese.
haloumi a Greek Cypriot salty sweet cheese with a semi-firm, spongy texture; ripened and stored in salted whey. Best grilled or fried, it holds its shape well. Eat while still warm as it toughens on cooling.
mozzarella a soft, spun-curd cheese. Has a low melting point and elastic texture; adds texture rather than flavour.
parmesan also known as parmigiana; a hard, grainy cows-milk cheese.
ricotta a sweet, moist, soft, white cows-milk cheese; has a slightly grainy texture.

CHICKEN
drummettes small fleshy part of the wing between shoulder and elbow, trimmed to resemble a drumstick.
drumsticks leg with skin and bone intact.

CHICKPEAS also called garbanzos; an irregularly round, sandy-coloured legume. Available canned or dried.

CINNAMON dried inner bark of the shoots of the cinnamon tree; comes in stick (quill) or ground form.

CORNFLOUR or cornstarch. Available made from 100% corn as well as wheat.

CORNICHONS French for gherkin, a very small variety of cucumber.

COUSCOUS a fine, grain-like cereal product made from semolina; from the countries of North Africa. A semolina flour and water dough is sieved then dehydrated to produce minuscule even-sized pellets of couscous; it is rehydrated by steaming or with the addition of a warm liquid and swells to three or four times its original size.

CUMIN also known as zeera or comino.

EGGS if recipes in this book call for raw or barely cooked eggs, excercise caution if you are at risk of salmonella food poisoning (pregnant women, young children and those suffering from immune deficiency diseases).

EGGPLANT purple-skinned vegetable also known as aubergine. Also available char-grilled, packed in oil, in jars.

FLOUR
buckwheat not a true cereal, but a flour is made from its seeds. Available from health-food stores.
chickpea (besan) made from ground chickpeas so is gluten-free and high in protein. Available from health-food stores and most supermarkets.
plain an all-purpose flour made from wheat. Also available as gluten-free from most supermarkets.
rice very fine, almost powdery, gluten-free flour; made from ground rice.
self-raising plain flour mixed with baking powder in the proportion of 1 cup flour to 2 teaspoons baking powder. Also available as gluten-free from most supermarkets.

GELATINE we use powdered gelatine.

KUMARA Polynesian name of orange-fleshed sweet potato.

LAMB, BACKSTRAP also called eye of loin; the larger fillet from a row of loin chops or cutlets.

MAPLE SYRUP a syrup distilled from the sap of the maple tree. Maple-flavoured syrup is not an adequate substitute.

MUSHROOMS
enoki sold in clumps of long, slender stems with tiny, snowy white caps; have a delicate fruit flavour and a soft texture.
oyster also known as abalone; grey-white mushrooms shaped like a fan. Prized for their smooth texture and subtle, oyster-like flavour.

NOODLES, HOKKIEN fresh wheat noodles, look like thick, yellow-brown spaghetti; needs no pre-cooking.

OIL
peanut pressed from ground peanuts; handles high heat without burning.
sesame made from roasted, crushed, white sesame seeds; a flavouring rather than a cooking medium.

ONIONS, GREEN also called scallion or, incorrectly, shallot; an immature onion picked before the bulb has formed, having a long, bright-green edible stalk.

POLENTA also known as cornmeal; a flour-like cereal made of dried corn (maize) sold ground in different textures. Also the name of the dish made from it.

PRESERVED LEMON RIND quartered lemons are preserved in salt and lemon juice or water. To use, remove and discard pulp, squeeze juice from rind then rinse rind well and slice thinly. Sold in jars or singly by delicatessens; once opened, store under refrigeration.

PROSCIUTTO an unsmoked Italian ham, salted, air-cured and aged; usually eaten uncooked.

PUFFED MILLET the smallest of all grains, it has a mildly sweet, nut-like flavour; is steamed then heated until it puffs up, similar to puffed rice cereals.

PUFFED RICE a type of puffed grain made from rice; usually made by heating rice kernels under high pressure.

RICE BUBBLES puffed rice breakfast cereal.

RICE FLAKES dehusked rice flattened into flat light dry flakes.

RICE PAPER SHEETS made from rice paste and stamped into rounds. Are quite brittle, but become pliable when dipped momentarily in water.

ROCKET also called arugula; a peppery-tasting green leaf.

ROLLED OATS oat groats (husked oats) steamed-softened, flattened with rollers, dried and packaged as a cereal product.

SAUCES
fish also called nam pla or nuoc nam; made from pulverised salted fermented fish (anchovies). Has a pungent smell and strong taste; use to your taste.
hoisin a thick, sweet and spicy chinese paste made from salted fermented soya beans, onions and garlic.
soy made from fermented soya beans.
japanese soy an all-purpose low-sodium soy sauce made with more wheat content than its Chinese counterparts.
kecap manis (ketjap manis) a thick soy sauce with added sugar and spices.
light soy a thin, pale but salty sauce. Not a salt-reduced or low-sodium soy sauce.
worcestershire a dark condiment made from garlic, soy sauce, tamarind, onions, molasses, lime, anchovies, vinegar and seasonings. Available in supermarkets.

SAMBAL OELEK an Indonesian paste made from ground chillies and vinegar.

SEMOLINA coarsely ground flour milled from durum wheat.

SHALLOTS also called french shallots or eschalots; small, brown-skinned, elongated members of the onion family.

SOY MILK a rich creamy 'milk' extracted from soya beans. It has a nutty flavour. Also available gluten-free.

SPINACH also known as english spinach and incorrectly, silver beet.

SUGAR
brown soft, finely granulated sugar retaining molasses for colour and flavour.
icing also called confectioners' or powdered sugar; granulated sugar crushed with a little cornflour.
pure icing also called confectioners' or powdered sugar, but no added cornflour.

SUNFLOWER SEED KERNELS dried husked sunflower seeds.

TOFU also called soybean curd or bean curd; available fresh (soft or firm) and processed (fried or pressed dried sheets). Fresh tofu can be refrigerated in water (changed daily) for up to 4 days.

VEAL SCHNITZEL a thinly sliced steak available crumbed or plain (uncrumbed).

VINEGAR
balsamic a deep, rich, brown vinegar with a sweet and sour flavour. Made from the juice of Trebbiano grapes.
cider (apple) made from fermented apples. Can be alcoholic or non-alcoholic.
rice a colourless vinegar made from fermented rice and flavoured with sugar and salt. Sherry can be substituted.

WOMBOK also called peking or chinese cabbage. Elongated in shape with pale green, crinkly leaves.

WONTON WRAPPERS sold in the refrigerated section of Asian grocery stores and supermarkets; gow gee or spring roll sheets can be substituted.

YOGURT we use plain full-cream.

ZUCCHINI also known as courgette.

conversion chart

measures

One Australian metric measuring cup holds approximately 250ml; one Australian metric tablespoon holds 20ml; one Australian metric teaspoon holds 5ml.

The difference between one country's measuring cups and another's is within a two- or three-teaspoon variance, and will not affect your cooking results. North America, New Zealand and the United Kingdom use a 15ml tablespoon.

All cup and spoon measurements are level. The most accurate way of measuring dry ingredients is to weigh them. When measuring liquids, use a clear glass or plastic jug with the metric markings.

We use large eggs with an average weight of 60g.

dry measures

metric	imperial
15g	½oz
30g	1oz
60g	2oz
90g	3oz
125g	4oz (¼lb)
155g	5oz
185g	6oz
220g	7oz
250g	8oz (½lb)
280g	9oz
315g	10oz
345g	11oz
375g	12oz (¾lb)
410g	13oz
440g	14oz
470g	15oz
500g	16oz (1lb)
750g	24oz (1½lb)
1kg	32oz (2lb)

liquid measures

metric	imperial
30ml	1 fluid oz
60ml	2 fluid oz
100ml	3 fluid oz
125ml	4 fluid oz
150ml	5 fluid oz (¼ pint/1 gill)
190ml	6 fluid oz
250ml	8 fluid oz
300ml	10 fluid oz (½ pint)
500ml	16 fluid oz
600ml	20 fluid oz (1 pint)
1000ml (1 litre)	1¾ pints

length measures

metric	imperial
3mm	⅛in
6mm	¼in
1cm	½in
2cm	¾in
2.5cm	1in
5cm	2in
6cm	2½in
8cm	3in
10cm	4in
13cm	5in
15cm	6in
18cm	7in
20cm	8in
23cm	9in
25cm	10in
28cm	11in
30cm	12in (1ft)

oven temperatures

These oven temperatures are only a guide for conventional ovens. For fan-forced ovens, check the manufacturer's manual.

	°C (Celsius)	°F (Fahrenheit)	Gas Mark
Very slow	120	250	½
Slow	150	275-300	1-2
Moderately slow	160	325	3
Moderate	180	350-375	4-5
Moderately hot	200	400	6
Hot	220	425-450	7-8
Very hot	240	475	9

index

o

p

First published in 2009 by Bauer Media Books, Australia.
Revised in 2010. This edition published in 2019.
Bauer Media Books is a division of Bauer Media Pty Ltd.

BAUER MEDIA GROUP

bauer media group

Chief executive officer Paul Dykzeul
Chief financial officer Andrew Stedwell

bauer media books

Publisher Sally Eagle
Acting publisher Simone Aquilina
Editorial & food director Sophia Young
Creative director Hannah Blackmore
Managing editor Stephanie Kistner
Designer Hieu Chi Nguyen
Food writer Xanthe Roberts
Illustrator Louise Pfanner
Operations manager David Scotto
Business development manager Meg Kennedy

International rights manager Simone Aquilina
saquilina@bauer-media.com.au
ph +61 2 8268 6278

Published by Bauer Media Books, a division of Bauer Media Pty Ltd,
54 Park St, Sydney; GPO Box 4088, Sydney, NSW 2001, Australia
Ph +61 2 8116 9334; Fax +61 2 9126 3702
www.awwcookbooks.com.au

Printed in China by C&C Offset Printing.

A catalogue record for this book is available
from the National Library of Australia.

ISBN: 978-1-92569-546-5 (hardback)

To order books, phone 136 116 (within Australia) or
order online at www.awwcookbooks.com.au
Send recipe enquiries to: recipeenquiries@bauer-media.com.au